Dennis M. Wilson

Copyright © 2017 Dennis M Wilson

Cover Design by: Aljun Majo and Jefferson Balorio

Photo Credit: Kiyokazu Watanabe

All rights reserved. The use of any or part of this publication reproduced in any form or by any means electronically, mechanically, photographed, modified or otherwise, or stored in a retrieval system without prior written consent of the author or in the case of photocopying or other reprographic copying, license Canadian Copyright Licensing agency is an infringement of the copyright law.

The MLM Success Bible: The Truth is Good Enough is a work of nonfiction. Nonetheless some names and persons characteristics of individuals or events have been changed to disguise some very awesome people. Resulting resemblance to persons living or dead is entirely coincidental and unintentional.

The publication is designed to provide accurate information regarding the subject matter covered. It is sold with the understanding that the publisher and author is not engaged in rendering legal, accounting, or other professional services. If legal advice or other expert assistance is required the service of a competent professional person should be sought.

Dennis M. Wilson, author, *The MLM Success Bible: The Truth is Good Enough*

ISBN-13: 978-1976491399

ISBN- 10 1976491398

Published in the United States by

Internetnextstep.com houraday.com

Other Works by Dennis M. Wilson

The Small Business Bible

The Cryptocurrancy Mining Bible

TABLE OF CONTENTS

Part 1
SETTING YOURSELF FOR MLM SUCCESS

Introduction	1
The History and Truth of Network Marketing	4
The Advantages of MLM over Traditional Business	14
What Makes an Effective Networker	17
My Attitude towards Network Marketing	18

Part 2
FACTS AND FALLACIES ABOUT MLM

Difference Between MLM and a Pyramid	22
What is a Pyramid Scheme?	22
Why MLM is different	23
The Gray Areas	24
Correct and Incorrect MLM Practices	26
The Commission Structure	26
Unilevel	26
Binary System	27
Matrix	27
What Could Go Wrong?	28
What It Takes to Succeed in MLM	30
The Truth about Lead Acquisition	31
The Truth about Downline Building Services	33
The Truth about Autoship	35
How NOT to Do MLM	36

Part 3

BUILDING YOUR OWN NETWORK

Choosing the Best MLM Company for You	39
Finding Your Business Partners	42
The Warm Market	42
The Cold Market	47
Conducting MLM Surveys and Presentations	48
The MLM Success System	52
The Approach	52
The Information	53
The Telephone 3-way Follow-up	54
A Modern Approach to Network Building	58
Finding the Right MLM Software	58
Choosing Between Ad-coop and Buying Leads	59
Checking MLM Membership Online	61

Part 4

PRESENTING THE OPPORTUNITY

General Rules of MLM Presentations	65
Lead with the Business	65
Commission Plan – The Simpler, the Better	66
Choosing between Flash and Powerpoint	68
Hotel MLM Presentation	70
Mechanics of the Hotel Presentation	71
Equipment to be Used for the Hotel Presentation	72
Hall Preparation	72

In-home MLM Business Presentation 75
    The 2-on-1 75
    The 1-on-1 75
Handling Objections 77
    Basic Steps 77
    Handling Objections about the MLM Business 79
    Handling Objections about the MLM Products 89

Part 5
ONGOING INCOME & MLM EDUCATION

Ways to Earn After Building Your Network 92
    Leveraged Residual Income 92
    Retailing Products with an MLM Software 93
    Residual Income through Your MLM Website 94
Learning More about the Business 98
    Second Life Virtual MLM World 98
    Second Life as a Virtual Training Ground 98
    How NOT to Spend Time in Second Life 99
    MLM University Training 100

Part 6
KEEPING YOUR EYES ON THE PRIZE

The Roatan Connection 103
The Pain and Pleasure of Prospecting 105
"Think and Grow Rich" 116
Don't Give Up on Your Dreams 118
Conclusion 120

THE MLM TRAINING MANUAL

Part 1

SETTING YOURSELF FOR MLM SUCCESS

INTRODUCTION

Successful MLM networkers didn't just happen by chance. Networking legends, the likes of Keith Halls, Nathan Ricks, and Randy Paul Gage, have shown to the world that MLM success can be achieved practically by any person who has the right mindset and commitment to learn how the industry works. It takes a lot of patience, and an open mind to accept new ideas. But most importantly, it calls people to action, to come out of their comfort zones, and to start working out – as soon as possible.

Networkers are, in many ways, like high-performance athletes. It takes practice and a lot of training. Oftentimes, they need to sacrifice more than what the average person is capable of, and be willing to walk the extra mile – learning about people; learning about the company, its products and compensation plans; attending MLM seminars and trainings, sponsoring downlines and building up teams; facing rejections and handling objections about the business, to name a few. But at the end of a long day, networkers can still put up a smile and be satisfied because they know their efforts are well worth it.

Knowing that multi-level marketing is well-grounded in sound principles and has long been in existence for more than half a century as a very successful and legitimate business model is quite reassuring for every aspiring networker. By looking back at the origins of MLM, we can fully understand how this industry came about and gain an appreciation in what this marketing technique can do for all kinds of businesses. These include an efficient system of product distribution, increasing reach through effective use of leverage and multiplication, and targeted leads by putting more emphasis on the warm market.

Becoming a networker expose people to a lot of criticism and being judged unfairly for bearing the semblance of pyramid schemes in which MLMs are never a part of, nor have anything to do with. Networkers need to be able to confront such accusations by delineating the difference between multi-level marketing and pyramid schemes, and bring to light some of the misconceptions about the MLM industry. Among these are the concept of lead acquisition, increased growth using downline-building services, and the often-debated topic about autoship. We'll summarize the most commonly used compensation plans, correct and incorrect MLM practices, and some reasons why most networkers fail at MLM.

The most challenging aspect of MLM is the initial stages of finding the right people and building their teams from the ground up which involves looking through long lists of contacts and calling them up one prospect at a time. Networkers should always aspire leadership in MLM by building their own network of distributors if they are to succeed in this industry. They need to have like-minded people joining them who share the same interests as theirs and work together towards the same goal. Networkers should learn to accept and embrace the reality about prospecting – that rejections and objections is part of the business – and handling such requires a constant state of readiness and a positive attitude.

MLM presentations are pivotal in any multi-level marketing engagement. The ability to convert prospects into one of the distributors hinges in this very crucial moment. Poorly done, the whole presentation will more likely confuse or turn off potential prospects instead of making things simpler and easier for them. Some of the methods that stood the test of time include the 2-on-1, three-way calls, and hotel MLM presentations, although few networkers still use traditional approach like the 1-on-1.

Multi-level marketing draws its strength from its ability to create long-term, reliable, residual income. It's the main reason people are starting to jump out of the rat race to become networkers. Leveraged, residual income is virtually non-existent in any kind of employment. The only exception are the top-level executives who doesn't have to do all the heavy-lifting and still be able to get the biggest share of the company's income. With MLM, every distributor, regardless of his position will experience long-term, leveraged, residual income by building up his own network of distributors and teaching them to do the same. This concept of leverage and duplication are two of the biggest secrets of MLM success.

Successful networkers knew the importance of training and continuing education in MLM. As one engages in multi-level marketing, he needs to keep himself updated with the latest developments in the business. Old ways of prospecting and business presentations will have to go, and they should start adopting newer ways which includes the use of modern technology, the Internet, and the social media. Multi-level marketing, like any kind of business, is very dynamic and constantly evolving. Some networkers, or even MLM companies came close to being wiped out by the competition or shut down by authorities for failing to adopt to the many changes in the industry.

It takes a lot of heart and motivation to succeed in MLM. By learning from the success of others, networkers can have something to reflect on and inspire them to keep going. Success stories in MLM are not made up. You can certainly have yours if you know how it's properly done. Read on, and set yourself for MLM success!

DENNIS M. WILSON

THE HISTORY AND TRUTH OF NETWORK MARKETING
by Greg Stewart

Enlightenment vs. 'En-darkenment'

The most fundamental fact of life in our world today is change. As a rule, people are reluctant to change. We resist it, we like to stay within our comfort zone of what is known and accepted by most. *This is human nature.*

But it's true that what you resist will persist, especially when you resist a better method whose time has come. In almost every field of endeavour, the arts, sciences, medicine, and business, most new ideas have always met with resistance and rejection at first. The more unique and revolutionary the idea, the louder and stronger the opposition to it.

People have always been afraid and even ignorant about ideas and methods that may result in change. Fear of change caused ridicule of Christopher Columbus, Louis Pasteur, Thomas Edison and Albert Einstein. There are other examples of how fear of change had effects on progress.

In the 1800's, people bought what they needed at small, family-owned shops. Then a man named W.T. Grant had an idea that created change. What if we combined all these separate, little shops by making them individual departments under one roof, in one large store? A new and better way of doing things. Customers loved it.

The individual merchants who owned the old-fashioned retail stores saw their businesses decline. The shopkeepers fought back politically. There were thousands of them with thousands of votes, and they lobbied for their right to do things the same old way.

They finally got the local and state governments to outlaw Grant's department stores. Eventually, Grant's department store won out. If there is a better way it will persist. In the early 1960's franchising was a revolutionary new technology in business, and it was also met with resistance. Newspapers and magazines wrote what a scam and rip-off franchising was. Stories of people who lost their life savings to some franchise were everywhere. There was a strong move to make franchising illegal. In fact, franchising actually came within 11 votes of being outlawed by Congress.

Today this so-called scam is responsible for over 34 percent of all retail sales in North America. Franchises sell nearly 800 billion dollars worth of goods and services today. Every industry goes through an evolution similar to this. Chiropractors were considered quacks in the 1970's, the stock market was considered shady and a form of gambling, and the first newspaper in British North America, The Public Occurrence (1690), was suppressed by the governor of Massachusetts. Now, we almost can't do without these industries.

The Pioneers

Like all-powerful concepts, Network Marketing has also met resistance due to a lack of understanding. There is no mystery to Network Marketing. It's just another form of sales and distribution. Network Marketing is 50 years young.

In the early 1940's a company named California Vitamins recognized that all their new sales representatives coming aboard were friends and family of their existing sales force, primarily because they wanted the product at wholesale cost. They also discovered that it was easier to create a sales force of a lot of people who each sold a small amount of product than it was to find a few superstars who could sell a lot of products.

So they combined those two ideas and designed a sales compensation structure that encouraged their salespeople to invite new representatives from satisfied customers, most of whom were family and friends, who each had the same right to offer the product and representative status to others, which allowed the sales force to grow exponentially. The company rewarded them for the sales produced by their entire group or network of sales representatives. Network Marketing was born! A few years later, the company changed its name to NutraLite Food Supplement Corporations.

In 1956, NutraLite was joined in Network Marketing by Dr. Forrest Shaklee to gain a broader distribution of the food supplements he had developed.

Not long after, in 1959, former NutraLite distributors Rich DeVoss and Jay Van Andel started the Amway Company as the American Way of marketing products. Like many truly innovative breakthroughs, the development of true network marketing was an accident.

Abuses of exponential growth haunted network marketing for years and it is still misunderstood today. One of the first abuses of the concept of exponential growth to generate income may have been the chain letter craze that swept the U.S. after World War I. The letters promised great profit if you would send a dime or a dollar to the person at the bottom.

The chain letters spread as far as Europe, and by the 1930's the U.S. post office estimated that 10 million letters were being mailed each day. Postal Authorities and law enforcement agencies battled the fraudulent schemes and the chain letter phenomenon began to subside in the early 1940s. Unfortunately, this scam spawned schemes which came to be known as pyramids, where money was given for the right to involve others, as no valid product which was being purchased from the company.

In 1974, Senator Walter Mondale declared such companies to be the nation's number one consumer fraud. Law enforcement agencies moved quickly to clean up the abuses. In the mid 1970's, with no clear understanding of what constituted a legitimate use of network marketing, the Federal Trade Commission and state agencies across the nation turned their eyes to almost all network marketing companies. In 1975, the FTC (Federal Trade Commission) filed suit against Amway, alleging that the company was an illegal pyramid and that its refusal to sell its products in retail stores constituted a restraint of trade.

Amway spent four years and millions of dollars in legal fees to clear its name. In 1979 the FTC ruled that Amway was not a pyramid; that its revenue was generated from the sale of its products, and the FTC acknowledged network marketing as a legal and efficient distribution system. Network Marketing exploded in the next decade.

Who's Involved in Network Marketing?

Today there are thousands of Network Marketing companies operating throughout the United States, Canada, Mexico, South America, the United Kingdom, Europe, Australia, New Zealand, Israel, Japan and the Pacific Basin. Little Malaysia alone has more than 800 active Network Marketing companies. Network Marketing is reported to be a $100 billion-dollar industry, internationally, made up of FORTUNE 500 and New York Stock Exchange (NYSE) companies.

In 1993, Amway was the fastest growing foreign company in Japan with sales over $1 billion. Discovery Toys markets their products solely by Network Marketing, with sales figures in excess of $100 million. Sprint, MCI and AT&T make their long distance phone service available through Network Marketing companies. The A.L. Williams Company utilized Network Marketing and astounded the insurance industry by outselling Prudential, a giant in the industry, in four short years.

Traditional sales method companies such as Colgate-Palmolive and the Gillette Company have Network Marketing subsidiaries. Rexall Drug is now utilizing the Network Marketing method of distribution with its subsidiary, Rexall Showcase. Network marketing companies such as Melaleuca outperformed Liz Claiborne, The Limited and John Paul Mitchell while Nu Skin bested the likes of Maybelline, Dow Chemical and Matrix. Mary Kay is bigger than Johnson & Johnson, Amway is bigger than Revlon, and Avon is bigger than Estee Lauder. Sam Walton, the founder of Wal-Mart is quoted as saying, "I'd rather run a profitable business in an unconventional industry than an unprofitable business in a conventional industry."

Network Marketing has evolved in other ways, as well. Companies that began as direct selling companies are now utilizing networking marketing compensation plans. Some examples include Avon, the $3 billion cosmetic giant, Watkins Products, which had been direct selling for nearly 100 years before it converted to network marketing, and Encyclopedia Britannica.

One reason for the decline of direct selling is that beginning in the 1970's, distributors making calls on people found that no one was home. Women, long standing as the customer backbone of direct sales, had entered the work force, leaving few at home during the day. Companies watching these societal trends moved quickly to revise their marketing plans to network marketing, which allows for more informal methods of sales and greater compensation.

Network Marketing Companies have pioneered entire industries: natural vitamin supplements, nutrition and diet drinks, concentrated and environmentally friendly household cleaners. One network marketing company almost single-handedly created the billion-dollar home water filtration business.

The Company Wins, too

Why are so many companies utilizing network marketing as their chosen method of marketing? Simply stated, it's more efficient! They do not pay for marketing, distribution, or sales until after the sale is made and the product is delivered. Compare that to traditional marketing where a company can spend millions of dollars on advertising, as well as all costs associated with an employee based sales force, such as benefits, support staff, communication, travel and office, before any product is sold.

Charles Givens, financial expert and bestselling author of Wealth Without Risk, points out that 80 percent of the cost of getting a product to consumers today is the result of marketing expenses. Companies are looking to move their cost as close to the point of sale as possible. Network Marketing companies replace traditional advertising and marketing costs with sales commissions to the independent representatives, paid after the product is sold.

In her bestselling book, The Popcorn Report, Faith Popcorn explains additional societal trends driving the success of Network Marketing. Her book describes consumers as having a desire to cocoon and stay at home. She believes that they wish to avoid crowded malls and traffic jams, and are looking for the convenience of direct delivery of the product that Network

Marketing provides. Advertising Age magazine states that the recommendation from a friend is the most powerful form of advertising; that is what Network Marketing is all about.

The changing work place has demonstrated that there is no security in the traditional corporate structure and career path. In the United States over 3,100 jobs are lost each day due to downsizing. Automation and technological advances are streamlining business and changing entire industries. Millions of people will be out of work searching for the same kinds of jobs their former employers just eliminated, in another company that just hasn't yet streamlined. This is postponing the inevitable; In fact, 47 percent of the companies that made up the Fortune 500 in 1980 are no longer in operation today, which represents a net loss of more than five million jobs!

Technological advances affect the work forces of entire industries. One example is the vinyl record business. In 1985, vinyl records supported a $24 billion a year industry. Today it is all but extinct, having been replaced withdigital downloads and streaming services . The steel and copper industries have suffered with the advent of new plastics and alloys. The functions computers are able to execute have caused the replacement of millions of workers.

Robotic technology similarly has taken its toll in the workplace. One robot can replace twenty human workers and extinguishes the need for companies to pay exorbitant amounts in employee benefits. Man Power Inc., a temporary service, is now one of the largest employers in the world because companies are finding it less expensive to hire temporary employees and thereby avoid paying benefits to permanent employees.

Marketing on a part-time effort can provide a financial cushion of residual income to protect oneself from such events. A recent Wall Street Journal survey found that 80 percent of the work force want to own their own business and 40 percent surveyed would like to work at home. This is exactly what network marketing provides. People are searching for ways to build a future that develops leadership and provides a balance in their lives for their families and each other, without sacrificing their sanity in the process.

How Does It Work?

In network marketing, you share information and develop personal and professional contacts. You are rewarded for sharing information that results in product sales. Network Marketing empowers you to build your own networking sales organization from your personal and professional contacts, which also empowers everyone to do the same, creating exponential growth of your network. You can earn income from the successful efforts of your network of business associates. Unlike conventional Corporations with one chief executive at the top, in Network Marketing everyone is the CEO of his or her own independent organization.

A network marketing company supplies the product. Then they join in partnership with a network of independent representatives, each one in business for themselves. The company takes care of the research and development, finances, management, public relations, production, warehousing, packaging, quality control, administration, shipping, data processing, the accounting and payment of representative sales commission checks.

Cooperation vs. Competition

One of the reasons for the success of Network Marketing in the 1990's is that it is based on cooperation, not competition. Unlike traditional business, career advancement in network marketing comes directly from helping to create success with those that you introduce to the company. Network Marketing is sharing information that results in product sales.

People involve themselves because they want to finally be compensated for what their efforts are really worth. They're involved because somebody cared enough about them to show them the awesome opportunity of network marketing. They get involved because they were ready to make a change. Why hasn't the truth about network marketing been told? People resist change and are fearful of what is not fully understood. People are comfortable with what is known and accepted by most.

The truth is that most people in power today have an overriding fear of the loss of their own power. Network marketing is about empowerment of the individual. Is it really your best interest they have at heart? Remember what happened with W.T. Grant, franchising, and the first newspaper? Most new concepts have always met with resistance and rejection at first.

Newspapers, magazines, radio and television earn their primary profits from their advertisers. Is it in the media's best interest to say anything positive about an industry that does not advertise? Do you suppose major traditional marketing companies that are receiving increased competition from network marketing companies are excited? Whose side do you suppose the media would take to protect their advertising dollar?

A few years ago a network marketing company that sold personal care products became the attention of the media and several state Attorney Generals. Their sales were approaching $500 million dollars. These sales were being taken away from companies such as Revlon, Max Factor, Estee Lauder and others in the health and beauty aids industry. Do you believe the competition was pleased with the success of a network marketing company that was not spending multi-millions of dollars on advertising as they had traditionally done?

Furthermore, network marketing companies were bypassing the department stores and malls and going direct to the consumer's living rooms with sharing, caring service and timesaving convenience. What if you were one of the brokers, retailers, wholesalers, media people or any other person whose job or businesses were being threatened because network marketing was a new and better way of doing things? What would you do?

If you had a friend in the State Attorney General's office, would you call them? If you or your company had contributed to any industry lobbyist, political action committee or had media contacts might they be contacted, too? What if, in fact, your job was in jeopardy either as the VP of Sales or as one of the executive staff who might have to answer to stockholders and explain why your market share was being taken away by some network marketing company and your position, your power and your income were at stake? Do you suppose these strategies are ever used against a competitor?

How many votes do you suppose an Attorney General would risk by focusing on a network marketing company that employed many people and paid a great amount of local and state taxes - in a different state?

Just as in any business or industry, there are scams and schemes that hurt the industry image. Real estate has had its scams. Banking and Savings and Loans have had their improprieties. Ministries have had abuses for self-serving purposes. The stock market has had its insider trading scandals. Why should network marketing be any different? Look at the company, the product, its management and their past history. Understand the commitment that is necessary to achieve success and residual income. This advice is just as valid in network marketing as in anything else.

There are many myths about the industry of network marketing and the companies involved. It is true that many recognized traditional companies have started subsidiaries, such as Gillette, Colgate-Palmolive, Rexall and thousands of other companies that are using network marketing as their preferred method of distribution, creating sales of approximately $100 billion dollars. It is often stated that Coca-Cola, Goodyear, IBM, Firestone, and General Motors are involved in network marketing with their own divisions. Actually, these companies are suppliers of products to companies that utilize network marketing, such as Amway. MCI, U.S. Sprint and AT&T supply long distance service to network marketing companies that are rebillers. Due to the high cost of real estate for showrooms, Toyota of Japan uses direct sales to market directly to the consumer, but not network marketing.

Network Marketing is the new way to financial freedom. You'll never create residual income and freedom from the traditional job. Even professionals are trading their time for money; if they are not seeing clients or patients, they are not getting paid. Most income is temporary and it is easy to determine if your income is temporary - just stop working for 90 days. If your income stops or slows down, you have temporary income.

In network marketing, you can stop trading time for money. Once you develop a solid network of sales representatives, you will create ongoing residual income. This can give you the freedom to do what you want when you want to.

It's interesting how resistant we are to change. We want to stay in our comfort zones even when we're miserable. It's been said network marketing is the next step in the evolution of free enterprise. But there is one thing we can always be assured of: the most fundamental fact of life in our world today is that change is inevitable!

THE ADVANTAGES OF MLM OVER TRADITIONAL BUSINESS

Multi-level marketing enables small-time, home-based entrepreneurs to compete with traditional businesses without spending a fortune on costly startups. It has also been a viable source of residual income for professionals and employees who want to engage in MLM business on a part-time basis.

In many instances, we have seen how MLM is more advantageous for most people, considering the amount of risk associated with starting up in traditional businesses, and the relative ease, cost-effectiveness, and leveraged income which characterizes most MLMs.

1. **Startup and maintenance cost**

   If you look at the risk involved with opening any type of traditional business – the costs associated with it and all the things you will have to do which you may not want, or may not be prepared for as the owner – MLM is a snap! In a traditional business, you will need a lease and office or retail space. It usually means at least a 3-year commitment, and a first-and-last-month rent up front. First-and-last-month rent will probably mean about 4,000 dollars or more.

   In MLM, you just need your bedroom or in-home office, computer, internet connection (if you're building the high-tech way; otherwise, a phone and fax will do) and a pair of slippers. The cost for all of that has already been covered once you have a place to live. In traditional business, you will have an additional phone bill and all triple net fees; in MLM, you're already paying for them at your house, hence no additional expenses incurred.

2. **Registration, licenses, and other paperwork**

   In MLM, you just have to choose a company, pay for signing up, purchase some initial products, and maybe do some advertising and promotion. This should cost you no more than 500 dollars in your first month, and maybe a couple of hundred dollars on your next month onwards. In traditional business, you're going to need startup inventory and business licenses, etc. which could cost you thousands of dollars.

3. **Stakes of losing the business**

In MLM you may be left with some credit card debt if you used them to finance your business, but it shouldn't be over a thousand bucks unless you did something wrong. In traditional business, if you fail, you would likely lose your house or any collateral you have used for your business. You could possibly be stuck with a lot of credit card debt if you used your personal cards to finance your business.

In MLM if you do not do the work and learn it, you would likely quit. You probably won't last 3 years as it is too easy to get started, and just as easy to quit. You don't need to wait for any leases to be up, or any other of the negative aspects of traditional business. In traditional business, it's even worse; you have an 80 percent chance of going out of business and losing everything within 3 years.

4. **Work-life balance.**

In MLM, you only fail in the business by quitting. So, don't quit. You'll eventually learn how to do it right and make a lot of money. In traditional business, no matter how good you are, your business can come to an end for reasons beyond your control.

In traditional business, you will possibly have to clean your own toilets, make your own coffee, makes sales presentations, deal with irate customers, deal with lawyers and accountants, and have to put up with a lot of your friends and family thinking you've lost your mind to start our own business. In MLM it is about the same.

As we can see, traditional business and MLM are about the same on the upsides, but way better in terms of potential downsides for MLM.

The Difference in Lifestyle

Some of the big advantages of MLM industry over traditional business is lifestyle. This doesn't necessarily mean big houses and expensive cars to most people. It may even just mean making the difference between your paycheck and daycare costs.

Let's say you're making 1,200 dollars a month working at a part time job and pay 600 dollars a month in daycare costs to enable you to do your job. That 600-dollar a month could actually make a difference when it comes to having the lifestyle you dream of.

Imagine not having to take your kids to daycare, but instead work from home and have a babysitter with them once or twice a week when you go to an event or some other presentation or engagement meant to build your business and income.

You could have your kids with you, make a little money on the side, and not have to deal with your kid's behavior which you might have to deal with in daycare.

For some, it may simply mean the ability to travel and build their own business as they travel. In case you didn't know, the tax advantages of doing an MLM business are simply amazing. This is probably my favorite aspect of being involved in this industry.

When I was away on a business related to MLM Software, MLM Training and MLM Tools (Japan, Australia, then back to Japan again) I had been away for almost 3 months. The negative impact on my income? Zero.

Lifestyle means different things to different people. You need to decide what it means to you, and whether or not joining an MLM business or work-at-home business can give you the lifestyle that you need, regardless of how small or big it is.

WHAT MAKES AN EFFECTIVE NETWORKER

Here is probably the biggest truth in Network Marketing or MLM: Success comes to those who are willing to do what others are not.

Here's a simple question. Are you doing something tangible that's going to grow you team? Training is fine, but the truth is that the only activity that will build your business is contacting potential customers or prospects, or doing 3-way calls with your team and helping them to do the same.

Everything else are simply just stuff that would make you feel better, but they actually have no impact on growing your team. This is the harsh reality about why some people don't succeed in MLM.

Get on the phone first, make the calls, and then move on to all the other stuff that makes you feel good. Action supersedes everything – that's my way of life.

Aim for at least 3 new contacts before the day is up. Get off the internet and get on the phone. Book a few appointments, do some follow ups or a few three-way calls.

There is no time like the present. Greg Stewart, a good friend of mine, taught me the power of 'action superseding everything.' Every time I called him for a little help, he would push me to get out my list and make a few calls with him before we even thought about training for the sake of training.

After we did a few calls, I found that I got my training done by just being in action. My enthusiasm was so high that I would work like a god the rest of the day!

Greg's way is the reason I ever cracked that elusive 10,000-dollar-a-month barrier. Let's get into action and start the ball rolling.

My Attitude towards Network Marketing

It seems every day I get calls trying to convince me that I should be actively building a network instead of building tools to help others build the networks. I do build networks – huge networks. I do this by helping companies put the tools and software in place to support all the people who are actively building teams.

I remember how it is just as bad when you're building an actual network and people are trying to break your belief in what you're doing in order to attract you to their opportunity. Isn't that tantamount to being told that your child is ugly?

I think it comes down to what some network marketers neglect – respect.

I will tell you a story about someone I know who has the most respect of other networkers that I have ever met. His name is Rick Jongkind, and he's with Melaleuca.

I met Rick about 23 years ago for the first time. He had responded to a fax campaign I had done while I was working with N/A/T/O International, an MLM company selling automotive additives. He was with Melaleuca at that time as well.

He responded to my fax and we agreed to meet knowing that we were both fairly focused on our respective business endeavors. Perhaps we could work as mentors to each other in the same industry.

We met, learned about each other, and had a very good cup of coffee talking about the industry. But neither prospected the other. We made the agreement to meet once in a while and promised never to prospect each other.

When my company closed, we met for the second time. I had the opportunity to take the top distributor role in a company called Teamglobe.com. I expected Rick to prospect me for Melaleuca more aggressively at this meeting; he didn't.

Instead, after hearing what I had to say about my position, he told me that I should take the top spot in the new company because he saw that it would be a great opportunity for me.

As it turned out, that company I started with closed due to a debit card provider stealing all the money of the distributors.

I joined yet another company with another mentor named, Greg Stewart (who I mentioned in the last chapter). That was absolutely amazing – 18,000 people in 4 months and over a million dollars in earnings! I never prospected Rick Jongkind, and neither did he prospect me.

That company ran into trouble which they eventually overcame. I decided to look for something stable at the time so I called my buddy Rick Jongkind. He never returned my call, so I left him another message. I was going to join Melaleuca and really wanted him to be the one to sponsor me.

About 6 minutes and 28 seconds later, the phone rang. It was Rick Jongkind. We agreed to meet and have him show me Melaleuca.

I got involved, built a fast team, and made about 5,000 dollars in my first month. Patience and respect – Rick waited 8 years for the timing to be right for me.

If more people in the industry would do this, we would all have much bigger success over time. Respect others in the industry. Stop trying to break belief in what they are currently doing. If you are so sure their thing is going to go out of business, then just be friends. When their thing is ready to go out for business, help them.

What I've seen is that most of the people who call me to try to convince me to do their deal now, end up calling me in a few months with the next deal. Why would I want to join with someone who pushes the flavour of the month?

Think about the damage you do to your reputation when you tell someone what they are doing is invalid, and that your company is the only

MLM company on the planet that is worth doing. Doesn't that invalidate our whole wonderful industry?

Let's start treating others with respect. Our businesses will all grow faster, and it may even help companies survive longer to provide that residual income we all desire.

Part 2

FACTS AND FALLACIES ABOUT MLM

DIFFERENCE BETWEEN MLM AND A PYRAMID SCHEME

Multi-level marketing has received a lot of criticism from several business institutions, self-professed marketing gurus, and misguided people who cannot properly distinguish between a legitimate MLM company and a pyramid scheme. Although we don't discredit the fact that some pyramid schemes are often disguised as a pseudo-MLM company, multi-level marketing in its pristine state is very much a legitimate and admirable business model.

Our goal is to establish the truth about MLM, dispel the myths about the concept of the whole industry, and be able to separate fact from fiction, so to speak. We're going to set the record straight once and for all, and bring to light the truth about multi-level marketing vis-à-vis pyramid schemes.

What is a Pyramid Scheme?

Contrary to popular belief, the concept of a pyramid structure when applied to business and government institutions is actually a sound one. In fact, every kind of business, or organization for that matter, operates in such a way. There has to be some kind of hierarchy in a corporate structure to function properly. Otherwise, every member in the entire organization would be working on the same thing – no one knows 'who does what' or who should call the shots. In this case, the whole system would be left in disarray and chaos would ensue.

A pyramid structure ensures that the company's resources and workflow are well-coordinated and are working towards the same goal. It was never thought of as a bad thing until a similarly structured scheme came along which also took the form of a pyramid. However, instead of distributing work and delegating tasks to generate income for the company, it uses a recruitment strategy to entice people to join in by paying people directly above them, and letting them do the same by recruiting others below them. This would later be known as a pyramid scheme.

A pyramid scheme is a form of fraud which carries serious legal and financial consequences. It has a pyramid structure like that of any legitimate company, but it is fundamentally flawed and unsound because the pyramid doesn't generate any real income and offers no value. Instead, it relies on membership fees drawn from new recruits, who would, in turn do the same thing. This process repeats itself until there's not enough recruits to support the whole pyramid and the whole thing collapses like a house of cards.

Why MLM is Different

Most MLMs also take the form of a pyramid, like other non-MLM companies. As explained earlier, the structure in itself is neither good nor bad. There's no such thing as a 'legal pyramid' or an 'illegal pyramid.' Think of another shape aside from a pyramid. Have you ever heard of people talking about a 'legal cube' or an 'illegal cube'? A fraud is a fraud, regardless of its shape. Nonetheless, the word 'pyramid' has had a negative connotation to most people because it is often associated with illegal practices, i.e. pyramid schemes.

Unfortunately, MLMs bore the brunt of this biased, stereotypical mentality. Just because a business model looks that way doesn't necessarily mean it's a pyramid scheme. Otherwise, we would have to call our government, or any organization for that matter, a pyramid scheme. A better way to look at things is to check whether or not the company is actually earning some money and not just giving them off to people whenever a new member comes along.

MLM companies are vastly different from pyramid schemes because they don't rely on recruitment to stay in business. It generates income for the company by incentivizing the use, promotion, and sale of its products and services. Traditional businesses have been able to accomplish these tasks by hiring salaried employees to do the marketing, sales, and logistics. MLM does things better for both the company and its distributors. Instead of the money being spent in all three of those, they become part of the compensation plan for each distributor which is way better in terms of earning residual income and promoting the business at the same time.

MLM companies use the concept known as 'leverage' in which distributors earn sustainable residual income by growing their own network of distributors who follows the system and replicates the process (hence the name, 'multi-level' marketing). Depending on your compensation plan, you might have to participate in the sales process and product usage to qualify for commissions, bonuses, and discounts. Again, it's no different from traditional businesses who spend money on people to market, sell, and deliver their products. In MLM, distributors are pretty much into business, but they also benefit from using the product or service and telling other people about it through their compensation plans.

The Gray Areas

The concept of multi-level marketing has nothing to do with pyramid schemes. The first company who came up with the idea of multi-level marketing used it to help them with the slow pace at which their products were getting sold. They stumbled upon the idea of providing incentives to sales reps who were able to recruit others to become sales reps as well. They came up with a compensation structure which will incentivize promotion, sale of products and recruiting more people who would also do the same. This came to be known as multi-level marketing.

Pyramid schemes also came up about the same time multi-level marketing was starting to flourish and was adopted by more companies. They also follow the same mechanism of recruiting others to find more people and repeat the process which, in their case, is represented by an endless chain. But instead of being used as a sales and marketing strategy, like what it was originally intended for in multi-level marketing, it turned into a fraud whereby people could exchange money for a position in the pyramid and make more money out of it. There's no real income in a pyramid scheme. It's a scam intended to cheat people from their hard-earned money.

Pyramid schemes would be easier to catch if they don't present themselves as MLM. By hiding behind the cloak of legitimacy, they are able to evade authorities and are able to spread and multiply in great numbers. They began to mingle and co-exist with other legit MLM companies leading people to the belief that they are one and the same. Sadly, this is the case with most people. Pyramid schemes disguised as MLMs also use products and services as a guarantee that the organization generates income and will be able to support itself.

But there's one catch. Most distributors won't be able to sell them outside of the pyramid because they're either overpriced, have no real value in it, or it doesn't create a demand. To qualify for commissions, bonuses, or discounts (and for the company to stay in business), they have to purchase a certain amount of product on a regular basis. This results in what is called 'internal consumption.' While there's really nothing wrong with internal consumption, it becomes a bad practice when you're trying to make a living out of it. It takes us back to the concept of a pyramid scheme – no real or sustainable long-term income.

Comparing MLM and pyramid schemes is like comparing apples and oranges. You can't say that one is better than the other, or say that one is a 'good pyramid' and the other a 'bad pyramid.' MLM is a legitimate and healthy business model, while pyramid scheme is a fraud. There is however, a good MLM practice and bad MLM practice which will be discussed in more detail in the succeeding topics.

CORRECT AND INCORRECT MLM PRACTICES

Networkers have had their own share of successes and failures. It's not a guaranteed pass that you're going to succeed in an MLM company just because it's already been established for a long time or has a very promising way of earning residual income. We'll look at some of the reasons why networkers succeed or fail in the MLM business.

The Commission Structure

The first thing you need to do before engaging in any kind of business opportunity is to understand how the system works. Don't be too concerned about the products yet or that you're going to end up selling or pushing them to people. You'll learn more deeply about them while working out in an MLM company.

There are different types of compensation plans but the most commonly used in MLMs include:

- Unilevel
- Binary system
- Matrix

Unilevel compensation plans reward distributors based on their own productivity. As the name suggests, your commission points would depend on the people directly below you but doesn't go deeper than that. In other words, you can only earn points from what your own downlines were able to make but not from people below them. There's no limit as to the number of downlines in a unilevel compensation plan. The more effort you put into it, the more you'll earn. Another advantage of unilevel is that you can easily manage your team because it's basically a horizontal structure. The downside of a unilevel compensation plan is that it doesn't have a mechanism to reward uplines for sponsoring people below their direct downlines. As a result, growth is typically slow with this MLM structure. Nonetheless it's considered the safest and fairest in terms of rewards and potential income.

Binary system works by limiting the unilevel structure to just two downlines ('left side' & 'right side') but has virtually limitless vertical development on both sides. In a binary system, commissions are computed by looking at both sides of the distributor's genealogy and rewards points based on the weak side of a pair across the left and right side. This could extend downwards in an unlimited fashion. As a result, potential income in a binary system could increase exponentially. Moreover, uplines would experience rapid growth by sponsoring a distributor below each downline. This, too, would encourage downlines to sponsor a new distributor to pair up with the ones whom their upline had already sponsored, thus earning their commissions on that pair. If each downline follows suit and applies the same strategy to people below them, their team would experience phenomenal growth and earn multiple figures in just a short period of time. However, this involves some risks since your income in a binary system would depend on having both sides working out. Otherwise, the team will stagnate and not be able to realize their potential earnings in using the system.

Matrix system closely resembles payment structures used in most pyramid schemes. As discussed in the previous topics, having the same payment structure doesn't necessarily mean that a company is a pyramid scheme. Pyramid schemes don't make real income and relies solely in recruiting new members. MLM companies, on the other hand, have positive, sustainable income based on products and services and cooperative effort of every member. As an MLM strategy, matrix system encourages rapid growth and supports an unlimited vertical commission structure like the binary system. Depending on the MLM company, they might have, for instance, three or five unilevel structures which could also extend several levels down. But unlike the binary system, it doesn't require pairing up to earn commissions, minimizing the risk of stagnation due to having a non-working side. In a matrix system, an upline can freely sponsor as many people as he wants below his downlines who could also benefit from it. However, he must exercise caution to prevent favoritism and some of the downlines feeling left out or disgruntled for not having his own 'share' of sponsored downlines.

What Could Go Wrong?

Like any kind of commission structure, MLM compensation plans are also susceptible to abuse. Let's take binary system as an example. In a binary system, some teams encourage the concept of a 'power leg' and use that strategy to attract more distributors, particularly the strong ones. An upline, for instance, will have a leg consisting of a 'powerhouse cast' (hence the term, 'power leg') and another leg (the 'pay leg' or 'working leg') waiting to be filled with anybody else. Usually, the pay or working leg consists of distributors who have never joined an MLM before. The strong leaders in the power leg will then fill out the pay or working leg to get their commissions while distributors on the other side do twice the amount of work.

In most cases, distributors in the pay or working leg are completely oblivious of what's happening on the other side, and some upline would even have them believe that they're in a power leg when in fact, it's the other way around. They'd encourage them to make their own power leg as well, just as what they've already been doing (in secret). While the practice of 'power legging' is not technically wrong, this strategy opens up a lot of opportunity for abuse (such as the 'binary game' explained earlier). It also creates a feeling of entitlement since being a part of a power leg, they won't have to do all the heavy lifting. Eventually, distributors in the pay legs become dissatisfied and would eventually leave the company. Rinse and repeat.

Other wrong MLM practices include:

- **Putting the cart before the horse.** Presenting the products and their benefits first before the business opportunity will almost guarantee a 'no' reply. Most people will distance themselves from people who try to sell them things. They must see this first as a very good business opportunity with you as a business partner. Otherwise, they can just be one of your buying customers. In such a case, you still end up with something and not walk away empty-handed.

- **Making unrealistic promises.** One of the reasons for MLMs having such a bad rap is due to networkers not living up to their downlines' expectations of an easy, unlimited, multiple-digit income they've promised them to have by just joining the company. MLM doesn't work that way. It's not some kind of a magical goose that lays gold eggs every 24 hours. The difference between MLM companies with traditional business is that each member in MLM has their own fair share of the leveraged income unlike in traditional business where only the top-level executives get the lion's share of the company's leveraged income. But the principle is just the same; you have to work for it.

- **Giving up too easily.** Many networkers are just inches away from realizing their dreams when they decided to leave the company. Success in MLM takes time. You need to fully understand the ins and outs of becoming a successful leader in your team and be able to make full use of the compensation plan and continuing MLM training to your advantage. As a business opportunity, you're investing your time, money, and effort on this. Don't give up halfway and commit yourself to it. Traditional businesses could take a year or more before they start earning positive income. Why should MLMs be any different?

WHAT IT TAKES TO SUCCEED IN MLM

What would it to take to become a successful network marketer? Would it be cheap, easy and fast? The answer to that is, it wouldn't be too expensive, simple, but not easy. And it's not nearly as fast as you think when it comes to increasing income, but certainly much faster than a job can create wealth for you.

Unfortunately, it's a shame that almost everyone in the industry claims that just getting into an MLM company will make people rich. We all know it's not true. So why drag the image of this wonderful industry underneath the ground by using this MLM pitch?

'There is no such thing as free lunch.' You can only do one of two things. You can either use money or time to make you more money.

If you have a lot of money, you can put that to work and it would make you more money. But if you just have enough, you can invest that into an MLM business, commit your time to it, and get wealthy. Then, as your income grows, you can put that to work and make even more.

It's about time companies start telling people the truth about what it takes to make money in the MLM industry. Let's be honest about it, and that it would cost them about 200 dollars a month to build a reasonable business over time.

Let them know they will have to obtain skills they don't currently have in order to make it and that it would definitely take a minimum of five hours a week, or an hour a day (seven hours a week) to have a chance of success.

They should know that if they're not coachable, it's going to cost them more and that it would take them more time to reach success.

What most distributors do these days is tantamount to telling people that they will make 100,000 dollars a year at McDonalds, skipping all the training and showing up to work only when they feel like it. It doesn't work that way. So why should MLM business be any different?

We have to be honest about the fact that people who give up quite easily shouldn't do MLM. They'd rather stay with their job making their wage and, quite frankly, stay 'happy' being poor. If we are to make good people interested in this industry, we have to be completely honest about it.

The Truth about Lead Acquisition

Perhaps the biggest myth in the MLM industry is that you can build a huge organization while using purchased leads for your autoporospecting system. We are of the general opinion that buying leads is an extreme 'last resort' method of building a large MLM organization, and that it can often lead to more heartache and loss than financial success.

Let's have a closer look at how companies generate these leads that are being sold out in the market.

First of all, they usually sell business opportunity leads only as these are the easiest to get paid for. They are also generated in a very generic way which means they can be sold to any MLM company or distributor.

Consequently, business opportunity leads are often used in a generic sense of looking for people interested to make some extra money with a home-based business. That is, if you're lucky enough and you're buying quality leads. Of course, you will never know until you've bought them, by which time it would have been too late.

Lead generation companies generate leads with online advertising, SEO (search engine optimization), classified ads, magazines, radio and TV commercials. But how exactly do these lead-generating companies make money if they are doing what you would do yourself if you didn't buy leads from them?

Advertising and lead generation is not a linear relationship. This means that if you can generate 10 leads with a 100-dollar advertising, it doesn't necessarily mean that a 10,000-dollar advertising would only generate 1000 leads.

Often online advertising like Google Adwords will generate far more leads per dollar spent than more traditional advertisement like magazines, mailers, and newspapers. Companies like my InternetNextStep.com, which sells MLM software, spends a lot of money advertising online, tapping into this higher-level advertising.

This in turn would bring down their per-lead cost, allowing them to profit by selling them to you for a seemingly competitive price compared to what you may pay per lead when placing your own local newspaper advertising.

This scaling of lead generation is unbelievable. There are even claims about a certain group who pooled their funds and spent more than 20,000 dollars for a one-page ad in Oprah Winfrey's O Magazine. It's a one-time ad, but it generated over 100,000-dollar leads.

This illustrates the point very clearly. Generating your own leads is more cost-effective than buying them if you have a big enough budget.

But it would only get worse. After all these leads have been generated, they are sold the first time as an exclusive and very expensive list. In most cases, you're completely clueless as to what kind of ad they ran to generate them.

Oftentimes, these leads are already thinking you're just a scam because of the way they were advertised. Days or weeks later, these leads are sold again, but not as premium as it was the first time. A few days later, it would have been sold multiple times as 'non-premium' and 'non-exclusive.'

So how do you go about this? The best thing to do is to call every premium lead you buy as soon as possible. Otherwise you'll be setting yourself for an extremely tough competition with many other network marketers who use the same method.

Here is where things turn out for the worst. Oftentimes, people who fill in forms and respond to such lead generation ads would do it en masse. In other words, they would fill in tens, or maybe hundreds of forms going into a lot of lead lists.

This means that even though the lead company you purchased the lead from is selling it as 'exclusive,' there are probably many other lead companies doing the same thing.

The solution? Call them – now. Not next week or next month.

The saving grace in this whole 'lead-purchasing' mess is that most people who are into buying leads are either lazy, too busy, or not paying attention. So if you have the time to take the abuse and call all your leads, you will likely be the only one to enroll people to your list.

The Truth about Downline Building Services

Ever heard about companies who can supposedly build your downline with one of their downline-building services? Do you feel excited about all the money they promised you're going to make without having to talk to your friends, family and neighbors?

Don't toss your money away for anything like this, because quite frankly, they don't work. The rule is here is, if it sounds too good to be true, it probably is. However, there are legitimate downline-building clubs as there are illegitimate hype-based systems.

Here are some tips on how you can tell the two apart.

If the company has a system to funnel raw internet or advertising-based traffic through an online sales funnel that you control, they may be legitimate.

If they tell you that you are paying for a share in an ad co-op where you get the appropriate share of traffic through your online system, and that if there's anyone who is interested you'll be able to get that lead to follow up with and see if they want to join your opportunity, you may have found a legitimate system.

If they tell you that they will do all the work, and have people sign up into your downline by just paying them a certain fee each month, then they probably are just another MLM scam of some sort.

Now it doesn't necessarily mean the MLM company itself is behind all these, but the downline-building club or whatever they call themselves certainly is.

If the company focuses on helping you to acquire leads through a well-established system, and offers a way for your upline to help you follow up with those leads and see who's interested, you may have a legitimate system.

Steer clear of MLM scams who offer false promises. Legitimate companies will teach you how to build your business one person at a time. MLM scams, on the other hand, will tell you how easy it is and that you don't even need to do anything.

Let's look at it from a mathematical point of view. An MLM-building 'club' or 'service' (so-called, overlay system, or any such name to make it look better) will promise you to find three people, and find another three people for each of them below you, and so on.

Hence:

1 person (you)	+ 3 person below you	= 4 total in the group
4 persons	+ 9 persons below Level 2	= 13 in the group
13 persons	+ 27 persons below Level 3	= 40 in the group
27 persons	+ 81 persons below Level 4	= 121 in the group
121 persons	+ 243 persons below Level 5	= 364 in the group
364 persons	+ 729 persons below Level 6	= 1000+ in the group
1000+ persons	+ 2100+ persons below Level 7	= 3000+ in the group
3000+ persons	+ 6000+ persons below Level 8	= 18000+ in the group

... and so on.

Each of the 18,000 plus gets three for a total of 50,000 plus, each of whom gets three amounting to 150,000 plus. 15,000 plus becomes 450,000 plus, to over 1.5 million, 4.5million, 15 million, etc. You get the picture.

Unless you came in first, it would soon take more than the population of a small country to keep their promise. Soon after, it would take more than the population of the world. In other words, there's no way these companies could ever keep their promise of getting everyone rich.

Real networking is different. If you build a team, you'll have income. Some people will build with you while some people won't. Some would stay as customers while others wouldn't. Some would quit and some won't. That's the reason why the mathematical model doesn't apply to a legitimate MLM company, as there are all types of people who get involved in it, each with their own individual goals.

MLM scams where you pay your money and get rich for doing nothing don't work. They don't do any good except making the wonderful industry of MLM look bad.

Find a legitimate company. Put in your honest seven to ten hours of work, spend time in your warm market, or spend a few hundred dollars a month on advertising and a legitimate sales funnel system to assess interest. Take a year or two to get good at MLM and you will be better off and feel good about the people you helped along the way.

That is the power of MLM.

The Truth about Autoship

Another myth that's been going on, especially from disgruntled networkers is the idea that autoships are bad for business. Let me set the record straight. Autoship is the way to go in almost any MLM that we know of.

If anything, autoship is the only way to make a residual income which is the main reason why we do MLM in the first place, and start building huge teams.

Suppose you built a team of 5,000 people and there was no autoship to speak of. How much do you think your check would be when you stopped growing? What if you stopped growing even for just a month?

Here's the sad part. You, and your whole team will have 'zero' income without an autoship every time growth stops.

Think of it this way. Why do you think a company with an autoship is a good company if it requires distributors to make purchases on a regular basis? What if your company doesn't require you to buy anything in order to earn commissions? You don't buy anything and neither does anyone else.

Consequently, if people stopped joining the company and purchase the mandatory starter pack of products, your commissions would grind to a halt.

Everyone who joins 'no-autoship' companies typically does so for the same reason. They dream of making money without having to buy anything themselves. In this case, likeness attracts. Soon they'll have 5.000 members who don't want to buy anything.

It would have been better to have 1000 people with a 50-dollar or 100-dollar worth of purchase for every person each month than to have 5.000 members who don't buy anything.

The point we're trying to make is this: no autoships typically means no commission checks, and companies that don't have one tend to go out of business and so does the MLM teams.

How NOT to Succeed in MLM

Dateline NBC made an exposé on Quickstar, Amway, Alticor, in one of their segments. They didn't try to taint the whole industry but just kept it to those companies.

There were a number of good things can be learned from that. Most of these were things you should certainly never do, or they're not even necessary for building a huge team with a reputable company.

I have seen the 'fake-it-till-you-make-it' type of person like the one on Dateline NBC saying he made 250,000 dollars a year in other companies. First of all, you don't have to be that 'big person' on campus to earn enough respect from others and encourage them to join your opportunity.

What's interesting was that he stated on National TV telling people how much he made and had the look in his eyes that he really didn't. But he was fairly desperate to make people believe he did.

So what's the dirty little secret of these companies? Most of the top leaders make their money selling sales aids, not their products. They even went so far as to say there is a chosen group of 20 at the top who control the sales aid business in their hierarchy.

But the saddest part is that of stories of people who did believe and lost their life savings chasing a very difficult opportunity.

The size of their conventions is awe-inspiring – a whole stadium full of distributors, lighting candles, passing the flame to two others or more like some sort of a ritual. It must have been a spectacle to see how fast a whole stadium could be lit from one candle sharing with two or 25 others. The truth is, we all dream of having our corporate conventions that big.

There's just one thing good I hope would come out of this story as far as our MLM industry goes. And that is that every distributor in any MLM company who watched this would feel sufficiently embarrassed over how foolish the person looked lying about his income, and that it would serve as a reminder to never do the same again.

It's interesting to note that he had a room with about 70 people in it. I have built teams, and I certainly know just how unlikely a person at the front of a room full of 70 people will be making 250,000 dollars a year unless his organization is somewhere far away from where the presentation is held.

Part 3

BUILDING YOUR OWN NETWORK

CHOOSING THE BEST
MLM COMPANY FOR YOU

Right now you're thinking how you can build a huge team in MLM. First of all, you need to choose an MLM company. Sounds simple enough. Your friend is into this thing that he or she is really excited about, and it seems like a good place to start.

Or is it?

We have a saying in network marketing: The first time you are in MLM your sponsor picks you; the rest of the times you pick your sponsor! It may be a good idea to join your friend, but it's also good to do some research on his or her company before joining. There is no 'right and wrong' for joining an MLM company. It all depends on your personal situation.

The truth behind network marketing companies is that 80% or more will go out of business within the first three years. Pretty scary, isn't it? But don't be too worried about it. The truth of any small business is that 80% of them will also go out of business in the first three years. Network marketing is not something magical; it's essentially a small business which is more likely to grow to a big business fairly rapidly.

So which one would you choose? Would you rather have a new business or an old, long-standing one? Making this kind of decision is not as easy as it sounds. Let's try to look at the pros and cons of both sides.

A new company is completely unknown, so everyone you'd talk to would certainly not have heard of it. This can either be good or bad. You will find whichever way you go that half of them will love the 'newness' of the company and the other half will hate the perceived instability of it.

A new company may seem a bit more exciting, but you do not have the 'stability story' to tell. In two years of working a new company, I loved the fact that it was new and fresh. But I also learned about the other half of the people who didn't like the fact that it was 'new' as they thought it may not be able to make it.

An old, long-standing company will have the stability but may not have the perception of being a good opportunity. Note that this is just a perception and is not necessarily true at all times. The truth on how good an opportunity is depends on how good you think it really is! Truth is whatever you believe to be true.

An old company will have stability, training, and systems, but you will have to fight it out since people you'd be talking to, more often than not, have heard of it before and have already formed an opinion. However, just because they've already formed an opinion doesn't mean it's always a negative one.

In two years of working an old established company, I found that 50 percent of the time the perception was neither negative nor positive. The actual name recognition of a good old company was fairly positive.

So how do we make sense to all of these?

Check on the company as to what quality of software they have, what the qualifications of the management are, how much capital they have access to (it's hard to get this number; a talk with the president will tell you fairly quickly if there is enough by how evasive he or she is on the answer to that tough question), and most importantly, who the top distributor in the company is and what their proven credentials are.

If the top distributor can prove they have built large teams in the past (don't be misled by a huge team in a binary; ask how many are on their weak leg as well), the next question is, why they left the company they built the huge team in.

If the answer is anything other than the previous company going out of business, tread carefully. If they left a company that still exists and continues to thrive, there is a good chance that they would also leave the company you are about to join.

The big problem when the top leader leaves is that the negative impression would be very hard to overcome. Often, they would also take with them any 'movers' and 'shakers' you bring to the team. Be extra careful if the top distributor in the company is an MLM junkie.

Join the right one, and residual income can be yours if you work hard. Join the wrong one, and the only residual you will have is the experience you gained in building your first MLM team.

FINDING YOUR BUSINESS PARTNERS

The Warm Market

Let me start with my own story in the warm market. The first thing I did – which I was right about – is I made a list. I made a list of 255 people. I blew through my warm market list in about 3 days. At least I didn't prejudge 60, or so, on my list. But I absolutely got nowhere.

The people I thought would be totally interested were not interested at all. I thought every single person would jump at the opportunity to buy our products. I was so sure everyone would support me in my new business venture. They didn't.

The difference was that the more people told me that I was 'losing it,' the more I knew I must be on the right track. The way I think of it was, if everyone agreed with me, then everyone must be doing it already, and that I wouldn't stand a chance making that much excelling at it.

I just went merrily along trying to drag them into watching a video or coming to a meeting. I pushed, sold, and tried to convince them to buy the products. Fortunately, I did sell all my products. However, I didn't get much interest in the business.

The one advantage to selling all your products as fast as you could is that you get all your money back and you can tell your friends about the profit you've already earned in your business. The second is the testimonials that you get as stories started pouring in.

At the end of it all, an uncle joined me in the business and a few of my father companies' employees did, as well. They only lasted about 3 - 6 months and never did anything.

I was not interested in following the system. For about one-and-a-half years I refused to follow the system.

Do you know what the system is?

First, I want you to think of one thing – duplication. The system has to be duplicable. After all the rejection in my warm market for not following the system, I deemed the warm market impossible and put the rest of my efforts into the cold market.

My thinking was that after making 5,000 dollars per month, they would be interested. Certainly not! After I got to the income part, they just said, "Yes, but it is one of those pyramid things. And you got in first. Of course you'll make it. I couldn't make it if I started now."

That really ticked me off after waiting two-and-a-half years to talk to them. Don't wait. Follow the system, and you will have success!

If you work your warm market properly with a simple system, you can see a lot of success. You might be thinking, "I don't want to talk about it with my friends and family!" But why? If you really believe in this industry and your ability to get to the lifestyle you desire, why would you want to do it with strangers instead of people you care about?

The first key to your warm market is to make your contact list. Are you one of those who claim to only have a warm market of 25 people? The most important thing you can do to ensure your success in MLM is to **take two hours right now and do your list.**

Think of it this way. If you only have five people on your list and two of them whom you just called gave a 'no' answer, how would you feel? What if you have 200 on your list and the first one said no? Does it feel a lot different?

Incredibly, we now have a mobile app that can cut that time down to just an hour by allowing network marketers to import contacts from both their phonebook and Facebook in order to start the process.

MLM List Builder by Internet Nextstep is one such example. It starts by jogging your memory to help you get the maximum no. of contacts for your list. You won't necessarily have to contact them just because they're on your list. But by forcing yourself to create a list, you're causing your brain to remember even more people, including those who would make your top 30.

The app allows you to rank your top 30 based on some very scientific criteria on who among your contacts are most likely interested in the business opportunity. Once ranked, you can transmit the list automatically to your upline for assistance and begin working on your future

MLM List Builder also has a feature that will notify your upline of your progress if you entered their email as your upline.

So how do we expand our list on the warm market? My rule of thumb is, if you can think of a name and put a face to it, they should definitely be on your warm market list.

However, just because you put them on your warm market list, doesn't mean you should contact them right away. The reason for putting them there in the first place is so that you can leverage them into a bunch of people they know for your list.

If you follow my list system, you may be surprised that some of the people you thought you shouldn't approach will show up at the top of your list once you put them through my ranking system.

Here is a list of people to consider that will put at least 35 warm market people on your list in the next 5 minutes. These will all be in addition to your family and friends. Now you can see how a list of 100 to 200 is taking shape.

1. Your Mom
2. Your Mom's best friend
3. Your Mom's other friends
4. You Dad
5. Your Dad's best friend
6. Your Dad's other friends
7. Your aunt
8. Your aunts best friend

9. Your aunt's other friends
10. Your other aunts and their friends
11. Your uncle
12. Your uncle's best friend
13. Your uncle's other friends
14. Your other uncles and their friends
15. Your brother
16. Your brother's best friend
17. Your brother's other friends
18. Your other brothers and their friends
19. Your sister
20. Your sister's best friend
21. Your sister's other friends
22. Your other sisters and their best friends
23. Who sold you your stereo or television?
24. Who is from your present job?
25. Who is from school or college?
26. Who repairs your car?
27. Who sells you suits?
28. Who is your financial planner?
29. Who sold you your home?
30. Who is on your Christmas card list?
31. Who is your florist?
32. Who runs your local gym?
33. Who sold you your automobile?
34. Who is your chiropractor?
35. Who is your local printer?
36. Who is your lawyer?
37. Who made your last family photos?
38. Who is in the Kiwanis club?
39. Who is in the Rotary club?
40. Who is in the Lions club?
41. Who is your UPS driver?
42. Who is your postmaster or letter carrier?
43. Who do you play tennis with?
44. Who are your children's friends' parents?
45. Who appraised your real estate?

46. Who is involved in civic activities?
47. Who is in your address directory?
48. Who is from your old neighborhood?
49. Who is from your old job?
50. Who does your dry-cleaning?
51. Who sells you fishing tackle?
52. Who is your hair stylist?
53. Who manages your bank?
54. Who is your accountant?
55. Who sells you office supplies?
56. Who do you play cards with?
57. Who do you play golf with?
58. Who heads your local PTA?
59. Who is your dentist?
60. Who is your family doctor?
61. Who lives next door?
62. Who has a booming business?
63. Who did you write cheques to this year?
64. Who sells you groceries?
65. Who is a waiter you know?
66. Who is a waitress you know?
67. Who teaches your Aerobics class?
68. Who is your minister?
69. Who is your jeweler?
70. Who do you bowl with?
71. Who is your travel agent?
72. Who sold you your eyeglasses?

Get the MLM List Builder mobile app on Google Play or iTunes and start managing your list faster, easier, and more enjoyable way. Take what you have learned and apply that to my list and ranking system to see where you should start. The best part is, as you grow your team you can have them use the app as well, and it will report to you who are actually coachable and worth your time to help and mentor.

The Cold Market

Here are some things you may or may not know about building your business in the 'cold market' – people that you absolutely know nothing about.

But before spending too much time in the cold market, it is strongly recommended to work on your warm market first. I had many distributors in my business who made a so-called warm market list and stop at 25 people. Before you can handle the cold market you need the training you can get in the warm market.

Online

1. Email Signatures - Anyone can use this simple yet powerful prospecting method.

2. Newsgroup or Usenet Signatures - This could make you spend a lot of time reading a lot of interesting information, but it's also a pretty effective way of promoting.

3. Free Classifieds - Submit to a bunch of free classified ad sites to generate traffic and leads.

4. Directories - Register your site with directory services relating to your industry.

5. Banner Exchange - Join a good banner exchange or start one.

6. Link Exchange - Get into a good link exchange program, or start one.

7. Search Engines - Register your Website with major search engines.

8. E-zine - Start an E-zine supporting your industry as a way to increase your customer base and establish your company as the leader in your industry.

9. FFA - Start your own FFA links page.

10. E-book - Write one on your industry.

Here are some forms of offline prospecting you may have heard of:

1. Surveys
2. Mall Cruising
3. Trade Show Walking

The best way to do offline prospecting is to do everything you can to direct people you run across to your autoprospecting site.

If you have gone back and re-evaluated the warm market as instructed in the warm market section, we can now get into a whole bunch of different ways to build this business with the people you do not know. These include:

- Flyers
- Classified Advertising
- Fax Blasting
- Email Blasting
- Answering Machine Messages
- Calling to Lists of Network Marketers
- Telemarketing
- Mail Outs
- Street Surveys
- Mall Cruising

Conducting MLM Surveys & Presentations

Is it possible to get free, high quality MLM leads? The answer can be as simple as asking them for a 60-second survey on just a few questions. As long as you have the will and the put your time to it, you can actually generate leads of highest quality – as many as you are willing to work for.

A street survey was conducted by team of marketing experts on the Streets of Vancouver, BC, Canada at the corner of Burrard and Georgia street – the busiest Street in Vancouver!

The instructions are based on real life experience conducting surveys for the entire summer, June to September, 7:30 to 9:00 in the morning, weekdays, on the busiest street corners in Vancouver, BC, Canada. Monthly income went from almost zero to around 10,000 dollars a month using this survey technique.

Here are some dos and don'ts of conducting MLM surveys:

1. **Don't say, "Do you have a minute?"** Nobody believes that anymore. Instead, ask if they have 60 seconds. Otherwise, you will have 90 percent less 'agree' to take your survey.

2. **Don't break your 60-second promise.** Don't be too 'chatty.' Get to the survey right away, set the appointment when you get one, and move on. You'll have more appointments to book if you don't dilly-dally talking to people who are interested.

3. **Do dress appropriately.** Choose the busiest street corner in your city with your suit and tie on, or its equivalent female business attire. Based on experience, wearing golf shirt and dress slacks reduced the number of folks agreeing to be surveyed by 50 percent when compared to wearing a suit and tie. It's been tried in actual surveys, and it really worked.

4. **Do go in pairs whenever possible.** Stand one on each sidewalk directly opposing each other. If the street side person can have a car parked behind them, all the better. Making folks 'run the gauntlet' will increase your survey count dramatically.

5. **Do pair up men and women if situation allows.** Generally, women book more appointments then men. The best pair is to have them both during the survey.

6. **Do repeat the same street corner for at least 5 consecutive days.** Try doing this for two weeks. By Thursday or Friday, many would stop out of curiosity. They might say, "Okay. Just what is this all about? You guys have been here for a week now, and I just have to know!"

7. **Do stay off of any private property.** Security guards will come at you and ask you to leave if your heels are on a big office towers property!

8. **Do check your local laws.** Make sure you are not breaking any of them doing a simple survey.

9. **Don't take product or samples while doing the survey.** There's always a proper time for that. Focus on surveying as many people as possible.

10. **Don't give any information about the company or products.** When booking your appointments, just limit yourself to getting as many surveys as you can. You will answer all their questions at the meeting.

11. **Don't run overtime on your meeting.** If you promised an hour, it should be no longer than an hour. No matter how interested they seem and how much they want to linger, tell them 15 minutes before the time is up that you have to get ready for your next appointment, or that you need to set another appointment soon.

12. **Do a balanced professional business presentation at all times.** Show a little 'pain' about the state of the world, the average peoples' income and life experiences, your company, the MLM industry, your products, your compensation plan, and most importantly, leverage. Your company should have an approved presentation to serve this purpose.

13. **Do try to book a presentation whether 2-on-1, Hotel, or Group Presentation.** Don't forget to bring this up to your upline so that

they can help you out. Although sending them to a website or some other "simpler" way of doing business is a lot easier to do, you will be rewarded handsomely for doing this business in a proper relationship-forming manner, especially when your competitors are doing it the other way.

14. **Don't let your 2-on-1 become a 2-on-2, or 2-on-3, etc.** Based on experience, the fact that you're presenting the business to a 'cold market' meant that one bad apple could turn off the rest. If, and only if, you're booking them to a formal hotel presentation should you group them together, and, in that case, 'the more the merrier!'

THE MLM SUCCESS SYSTEM

The MLM 3-step Success System is a very simple method and only takes a little of your time to implement every day. The three steps are as follows:

- Step 1 - The Approach
- Step 2 - The Information
- Step 3 - The Telephone 3-way Follow up

The Approach

Use this approach if your company is online. Simply call up your contact or strike up a conversation with following questions:

"Do you use the internet?"

"Are you making money on the Internet?"

"Isn't it amazing how many people are making money on the Internet nowadays?"

"Would you be interested in learning how you could make money on the Internet?"

At this point, Step 1 has been completed. If you got a 'yes' to the last question, simply ask for the prospects' telephone number and email address, and inform them that you will send them something by email on the next day or so.

If you're doing this personally and they don't have an email, ask for their phone number. If you have an auto-prospecting system of some sort, by all means give them your site information and get them to check out the website. Be sure to inform them that you will follow up with an associate to help answer their questions in the next day or so. The purpose of Step 1 is not to recruit but only to set up an appointment with them.

If they ask you to mail them something by snail mail, say to them politely that you don't conduct your business that way, and that you're looking for online, connected, ambitious people.

The Information

The information you send them by email is, again, very simple. Below is an actual sample email which you can use. With some sort of auto-prospecting system you will be able to incorporate this into auto-responders and reply to them automatically.

Sample Informational Email

Dear <Name of prospect>,

John and Jane Doe here! It was nice speaking to you the other day. As I promised I am sending you a bit of information on how to Have Fun and Make Money on the Internet. What an exciting place!

The support systems this company have to ensure we can build a great business and have fun with an hour-a-day of effort are simply amazing.

Check out my website at:
<Your website, corporate, or prospecting site URL>

It shouldn't take more than 30 minutes of your time. If you love what you hear, you'd be listening for more within that period of time. If not, you'd be done much quicker. I'm pretty sure you'll agree that it's well worth it.

I will follow up with you with an associate in the next few days to get your opinion about it.

Your Friend,
John/Jane Doe

555-555-5555
john@jane.doe

Remember to keep it super simple.

You can use any automatic prospecting systems built in auto-responders to get this information from them, and be able to send more timed follow-ups as well. An automated prospecting system can help a lot with both online and offline approach to building your business.

The Telephone 3-way Follow-up

This is the most important part. Not doing so sets you up for an almost certain failure. 'Three-ways' can be done by telephone, or online. In both cases be sure to enlist the help of your upline.

The key to a successful information referral of any kind is setting up the 3-way call when you hand out the information. If you are not keen at telling them that you will get back with someone you work with to handle their questions, you need to reconsider your stance about prospecting in MLM.

I'm a little bit uncompromising when it comes to this part. And for good reason. I've been through this myself before when I got started.

I told myself, "I am not going to let my upline talk to my friends and family on a 3-way call. No sir. He could mess things up!"

Or, "My friend is going to be so interested; I don't need my upline on a 3-way call for this one!"

The turnout if you do not use your upline would be something more like this. Your friend is not interested. He already knew of someone who had been burned by one of the pyramid deals. He launches into you about how foolish you are for getting duped into one of those things. The truth is, he had never even looked at a legitimate network marketing company. Everything he said about MLM were merely hearsays.

You know better. You have seen the light, and are very excited to tell him about it. The more he tells you that he is not interested, the more you try to convince him that he is wrong. And the more you try to convince him that he is wrong, the more he believes that he is right! Soon enough, the entire conversation deteriorates into an 'argument vs. poof', which then puts you a step closer to being a charter member of the NFL ("No Friends Left") club!

Your up-line can help prevent this scenario through a 3-way call because he is a neutral third party. He is not emotionally tied to the outcome of the conversation. He would be more willing to tell your friend that it is not for him if he cannot dig out and successfully deal with the objection.

You'd probably think, "Fine, as long as my up-line knows what he is doing. But what if my upline messed up the call?". The best part of the 3-way call is that, if your upline messed up, you can always call your friend back and tell him that you're sorry for what he did, and that you didn't know he was going to do that. Tell him that if somebody with no class like him can do business, you could probably do even more." It's hardly that you would ever lose in a 3-way call.

The 3-way call completes what is known as the 'Trust-respect Triangle.' Your friend trusts you, but probably doesn't respect your knowledge about MLM. The upline is unknown to your friend. Regardless of whether your upline is a successful networker or not, your friend would immediately respect his knowledge of MLM. This is simply human nature.

This little story about myself proves how deep this trust-respect principle goes into human nature. I obtained my Private Pilots license at the age of 19 (a dream I had, set a goal to, and went after). I took my buddy Kevin flying one day. Everything seemed fine. After we landed, he told me that it was the scariest thing he had ever done in his life.

Understand this. It was not the small aircraft that spooked him. His uncle had a small airplane and he had flown with his uncle lots of times. What got him was that he had to fly – with me. He told me he would rather have flown with a pilot he didn't know who is half my skill and training than to fly with me. But he did so, anyway.

The reason? He trusts me with his life. But he didn't respect my knowledge of how to fly an airplane. After all, I was his buddy that he partied, and had fun with. What the heck did I know about flying airplanes? But that's human nature, and we can't change it. We just have to learn how to work around it.

To do a three-way call, you need to activate the feature first with your phone company, or in most cases, you will be charged a per-use charge which can be somewhat prohibitive. Upon activation with your phone company, you will be charged a fixed monthly rate of just a few dollars.

When doing a 3-way call, start by calling your up-line (Note: this is a scheduled call as opposed to a random cold call.). Your upline will ask you a few questions about the person. Here is the information your upline needs to know. This should come in handy for each person you are going to call:

1. The person's name

2. What information the person has so far

3. The objective of the call

4. Whether this person been 3-wayed before and with whom

Once you have briefed your up-line with this information, simply push the "flash key" on your phone, or do a brief split-second hang up. You will hear three beeps then a dial tone.

Dial the person you are trying to reach. As soon as it starts ringing, hit your "flash key" or hang up. This will connect your upline back in. While the phone is ringing, quickly ask if he is there.

Start the call by respecting your prospect's time.

Usually, I would say something like, "Hi Fred, its Dennis Wilson calling, did I catch you at a good time?"

If your prospect says, 'no,' end the call immediately after giving you a better time to call back.

Always preempt by saying, "Oh, sorry," "How about calling you back in an hour or so?" This allows you to get it done sooner rather than later. If you ask them when you should call back, it's almost certain that they would tell you, 'next week.'

If he says, 'yes,' introduce your upline on the 3-way call, by simply saying, "Like I said when I gave you my website, I took the liberty of having <your upline's name> on the line with me in case you had any questions. <your upline's name> is already successfully working the business and will be helping me to do the same. <prospect's name>, meet <upline's name>."

If you are the knowledgeable upline, open the conversation by saying, "Hello, it's good to meet you over the phone. <distributor's name> tells me that you're doing a great job in the <industry they work at> industry – is that right? That website you saw looks really interesting, isn't it? Well, <prospect's name>, let me ask you a question. Based on the information you have seen so far, does it look like something you see yourself participating in?"

If you get a 'yes,' you can help to get them started right there, online.

If you get a 'no,' then obviously they have some objections. For more detailed discussion on handling objections, turn to Chapter <no.> about "Handling Objections."

A MODERN APPROACH TO NETWORK BUILDING

Many MLM companies start with inadequate MLM Software systems to back them up. As companies experience exponential growth, which is typical to the industry, their MLM software would not be able to keep up and the whole thing crashes and teams get wiped out.

When looking for an MLM opportunity, make it a point to check on the MLMs software and website. If it looks flashy, or is riddled with errors, you may want to seriously consider whether being involved with that company is worth your time and effort.

Finding the Right MLM Software

Our years of experience in MLM consulting business and MLM software proved just how important this information is as we have helped a number of clients transition from their MLM software that can't keep up to an MLM software that can.

Not all MLM companies are created equal. If you were able to pick a company that has been capitalized well enough to last, and has the MLM software systems in place to support your team's growth, you'll have a better chance of reaching your dreams of residual income.

So how exactly does an MLM software help the company and its distributors?

I think you will agree that sometimes it is hard for people to join an MLM because of the monthly requirement for autoship? Let's say you have web hosting as a product available from your company. If you already have a website, you could simply switch it over and those points would count in your commission plan.

How clever can that be? That thing you've already been buying, you're getting it from your MLM Company instead of redirecting your money. In other words, you're spending money for that business that's making you rich.

Automatic prospecting systems like CRM Plus can help build your business by harnessing the power of the Internet and all the wonderful sales and prospecting automation it can provide. What if that same product that helped you do it also counted towards your monthly commitment to products?

An automated Help Desk and FAQ engine can help your team more efficiently by letting them ask questions from you and have your answers go straight to your team support site for all of your team members to access. By answering a question once, your whole team gets the benefit of the answers instantaneously.

How about a shopping cart system that you can use to sell training materials to your group? Think of other products you can avail in other non-MLM businesses that you would like the public to have access to. Again, these products could possibly count as points in your commission plan.

Choosing Between Ad-coop and Buying Leads

When trying to achieve MLM success with an auto-prospecting system, network marketers must often make a decision between buying leads and generating their own.

Which is actually better?

While buying leads can give you tons of contacts on a plate, generating leads through advertising co-op may require a little bit of effort. But the quality of leads is significantly better. Besides, nothing worthwhile is ever easy.

If you run an ad co-op, or if you're lucky enough to belong to an MLM company that runs one on your behalf and lets you partake in it, you're on your way to riches.

Predominantly, the difference is that running an ad co-op or getting involved in one specific to your company and products, you will get a much higher quality of lead.

The reason is that ad approach can be fined-tuned to be much more specific to the advantages of your company and products as opposed to the generic 'shotgun' approach lead-selling companies are forced to use.

An ad co-op is simply a method of generating leads in which many members contribute a small amount of money each month that gets pooled for smart advertising aimed at generating high quality leads. Done properly, an ad co-op will generate high quality leads directly into a full-featured autoprospecting system which will do the heavy lifting for you.

How does buying leads turn out compared to ad co-op in terms lead quality?

If you've ever purchased leads – even expensive ones – you may have had the unfortunate experience of calling a hundred people, taking a lot of abuse, spending a fortune on long distance calls, and ending up with two or three new members or product sales at the end of it. If you've bought cheap ones, you probably won't even have this positive of an experience.

A well-planned autoprospecting system is the complete opposite of what lead-selling companies have been doing. They make a lot of money selling tons of leads, and they have very open ad campaigns encouraging people to provide them with some basic information and they might get rich or retire, or any such method to collect data from them.

With an ad co-op and autoprospecting system, the approach could be somewhat similar, but before even asking the prospects to fill out a form and provide specific information about themselves, they would be put through a sifting and sorting process to see if they qualify.

We call this 'exclusionary prospecting,' vs. 'inclusionary prospecting.' This simply means that a properly done autoprospecting system will make all the tire kickers go away and not give you their information, and you will have way fewer leads to chase around.

This would seem like a bad idea. Or is it?

The good news is, if you had a thousand people go through a properly done autoprospecting system and end up with just 25 good leads, you would likely enroll 50% or more of them.

These 25 leads whom you're about to call are already familiar with what you do, have answered survey questions to show their intent, and are literally waiting for you to call them because they are interested.

Compare that to lead-selling companies with the same scenario. They get a thousand people to their capture page, and they would try to obtain information about them while telling them literally nothing. This might give them 250 leads and sell them to you.

The next part is where it gets interesting. Out of the 250 leads, 25 are good ones, and would lead to the same 12 or 15 folks enrolling in your company or buying your products. The problem is, you need to actually call all 250 people just to find them.

Let a system do the heavy lifting.

This myth about getting rich buying leads and calling them is done. A properly done ad co-op linked to an exclusionary autoprospecting system will offer considerably better chance of success than simply buying leads.

Checking MLM Membership Online

How often do you have some unknown caller on the phone trying to convince you how fast their company is growing and going wild, and how you are missing out being in that company you are currently in. These are the kind of people who make the MLM industry look bad.

What if we can show them up something that would turn the tables on them? Alexa toolbar will help you do just that. It gives you the approximate rating of a website by way of a percentile basis.

It tells how a website ranks on the Internet. For example, if your website's rank is 99,345, it means that you are the 99,345th most looked at website that day along with ninety-nine thousand others below you.

Alexa toolbar enables you to take a look at the so called 'next hottest thing' and find out if that marketer who's trying to break your faith is for real or not. There's also a 'wayback' machine that allows you to see how the site they've been talking about looked like back then.

You can ascertain whether the opportunities being thrown at you are true, and at the same keep an eye on your own opportunity using just the toolbar. In my experience, an Alexa toolbar ranking of about 125,000 means the site is getting about 170 unique visitors per day.

So the next time someone tells you how great their opportunity is, and how explosive the growth they are experiencing, don't hesitate to use the toolbar. Bring up their website and see for yourself if they are giving you honest to goodness information.

If a company has 500 active members, they probably have 300, or so, unique visitors a day just on the involved members checking out their members lounge (if the company has good MLM software that gives them one).

Check out and look at the daily stats and three months back. Alexa will show you whether their claims of phenomenal growth is true or not. If they are not under 125,000 Alexa toolbar rating, you can bet their growth is meant to be explosive after you get involved and work your heart out for them.

Part 4

**PRESENTING
THE OPPORTUNITY**

GENERAL RULES OF MLM PRESENTATIONS

Lead with the Business

Unlike in traditional business, you will have greater success in MLM approaching people on how to make money rather than how to save money with the benefits of your products. In fact, product moves as a result of showing the business.

Most Distributors' belief is strongest in the product and weakest in themselves and the industry of Network Marketing. Hence, they would attempt to build their network as fast as they could by approaching prospects with the product rather than showing the concept of leverage and the sales compensation plan.

Think about this for a moment. The first time you were presented with the opportunity, did you lose sleep with excitement over network marketing thinking about the wonderful product, service or membership you were buying? Or, like most people, did you get excited about the possibilities of having a few friends join you in purchasing the product which could grow to a lot of people purchasing the product and create a residual income?

I'm quite sure that's not the main reason you've got into the MLM business. So why spend a lot of your time attempting to grow the network by selling the benefits of the products? When presenting the business opportunity to people, we should always talk to them about making money instead of saving money.

Here's the philosophy as to why showing the product first can actually result in less product sales than showing the business at the outset. When the product is shown first, people tend to move away and have negative thoughts about the MLM industry.

Most of the time, your friend, whom you're trying to sell things, is afraid to be honest with you about the products because it might hurt your relationship. He knew one of those pyramid schemes, and he might think you're about to tell him about how great the products are, and that you are going to try to sign him up in one of those pyramid deals, which he absolutely hates.

As you can see, he has no other choice but to tell you the products are not that good, which will slowly erode your belief in the system.

On the other hand, if you were able to present the business to him properly, you will also do a good job of showing the products. But if in case he's not interested in the business, he is more likely to buy the products without the above concern.

If he really likes the products that he wants to share his business with others, he may just come around to the business concept. By presenting the business opportunity first, we have absolutely nothing to lose and we have everything to gain.

This issue of whether or not we should begin with the product or with the business opportunity is among the hotly debated issues in the industry. All I can say is that in my 20 years of experience, the big earners I've met – people earning 100,000 dollars per year – all of them lead with the business while on the other hand, a number of people who argue with me about leading with the product, none of them are big money earners.

If you're interested in doing business presentations, there are basically four types of presentations you can do yourself or take part in which will be discussed in the succeeding topics. Of course, you can also use the telephone, the internet, and your teachmoney.com system to grow your business.

Commission Plan – The Simpler, the Better

The topic of commission plans in MLM is a crucial one. Here is the truth about it. Regardless of the commission plan your company has, your job as a distributor is to make sure you learn how to explain it in as simple and as quickly as possible. Put another way, it should be simple enough that even a seventh grader can understand what you're talking about.

Melaleuca probably has one of the most difficult to understand MLM compensation plans in North America. In the hands of an unskilled distributor, explaining it can become a dreadful experience. The good thing about Melaleuca's compensation plan is that if you know exactly what you are doing, explaining it would be much easier.

It's worth knowing that your prospect doesn't really care about all the specific details right off the bat. Don't spend four hours explaining it from the outset. Other compensation plans can be as difficult as Melaleuca's but they all seem to exhibit the same features.

The basics can be explained quite simply. For instance, Melaleuca uses a 5 x 7 Matrix with a lot of override bonuses. Simple enough. Your compensation plan may be exactly the same. You just have to find a way to explain it in simple language that is truthful and not misleading.

If the prospect asks about the override bonuses, speak to them in general terms, except when they're asking for more specific information. Take your prospect's — if they ask detailed questions, give them detailed answers.

With this approach you'll find that most of your prospects aren't too concerned about the finer details since they can get those once they are already involved in the business and start to get more training. But by allowing your prospect to take the lead, they can still walk from it and feel satisfied not realizing that you've held back some of the 'company secrets.'

Most importantly, don't exceed one hour for your initial presentation. If you go past the magic one hour time limit, you might expect something like, "It looks great and all. I appreciate how you can afford to drive across town in rush hour traffic to meet with me and spend three hours talking. Unfortunately, I simply just don't have that much time, so I can't do this business right now.

Choosing Between Flash and Powerpoint

One of the most important things your MLM company needs to become successful, in addition to a great MLM software, is a catchy MLM presentation, whether it's a spectacular flash MLM presentation or a splendid Powerpoint MLM presentation.

There's a lot of debate whether an MLM Presentation should be made as a flash MLM presentation or as a Powerpoint MLM presentation. I believe having one of them is a lot better than not having a presentation at all. However, it's also a good idea to have both. Here's why.

A Powerpoint MLM Presentation can be easily used to burn slides for traditional slide projectors for use by your members in hotel presentations. It can also be published on the web, although MLM flash are much more suited for this.

A flash MLM Presentation is a fantastic tool for promotion on the Internet and can have your voice and music added quite easily without compromising download and playability speeds. They can also be written on CDs or DVDs for members to use even without an Internet connection.

Companies like Internet Nextstep have extensive experience in developing MLM Presentations whether it's a simple Powerpoint MLM presentation, flash MLM presentations, or a more elaborate Powerpoint MLM presentations, or flash MLM Presentations.

One of the biggest mistakes people make when creating MLM Presentations is that they focus too much on their company and their products and leave out the 'pain points' of not having such.

The truth of any sales presentation, whether it's an MLM presentation or not, is you have to develop need. Incredibly, a lot of MLM companies create presentations all about their company or how great the company and their products are.

Without first creating a need for your product and concept, your prospects will never get to the part of how great your products and company are.

Here are some examples of how MLM consulting firms like Internet Nextstep were able to help their clients.

When vacation came along, the marketing side decided to have a complete walking, talking, interactive, and more elaborate animated flash MLM presentation. They didn't work on the content, but instead reworked on an existing Powerpoint presentation supplied by the client and went from there. The result was a nice and catchy presentation with animated characters that resembled the President and Vice President of the company.

HOTEL MLM PRESENTATION

The Hotel presentation is the big 'kahuna of showcases'. This may come as a shock to you, but hotel MLM presentations is not an absolute necessity to build a network marketing business. In fact, you can build a huge business just from having a chain of home presentations. Those who can't afford a hotel presentation will find this to be more duplicable, and easier to do.

That said, there are plenty of benefits that can be had from a hotel presentation. One key element is excitement. Once you're able grow to over 20 distributors regularly, i.e., weekly, going out to presentations, you may be ready to move to hotel presentations.

Check the prices very carefully. We don't want losing money in the process, and we want to be able to recoup most, if not all of the hotel fee. Charging 5 dollars per distributor at the door, for instance, will do just fine.

I'll take this opportunity to address one key issue I have seen with most people which they've been doing wrong for quite some time. Are you agreeable to the idea that successful people are the best ones to sponsor into your business, or that the unemployed make the best prospects?

Would you expect an executive type of person with all the interpersonal skills essential to network marketing to be your best prospect? You bet it is. An executive type of person won't be impressed with a meeting that starts late and is full of people dressed only in jeans and t-shirts.

When we became too lenient with our dress code, I had lost some valuable prospects who just couldn't see themselves participating in a meeting with so many 'unprofessional-looking' people.

Would you rather impress the executive types that have the skills built in, or the one who complains that if he has to wear a suit, he just isn't going to come?

The point we're trying to make here is that we should 'dress for success.' We must have a dress code and enforce it. Also, we need to remember to respect people's time by starting on time.

Mechanics of the Hotel Presentation

- Arrive early. Invite your guest to be there 15 minutes prior to the presentation starting time.
- Dress for success – and that means wear your business dress. If you 'dress for less,' you might have a bad impression to the group.
- Bear in mind that the presentation is intended for new guests. Your excitement must be the same the first time you've gone to the presentation.
- Distributors are as important as the speaker. Each member plays a major role in setting the tone and energy of the presentation.
- The same presentation is given every single time, because it works. Sit in one of the first three rows with your guests so that any distractions are behind you.
- Refrain from talking during the presentation and focus your attention towards the front.
- Do not distribute material during the presentation. If you hand your guest a catalog prior or during the presentation, they won't be able to focus on the speaker, and they would miss important concepts.
- Never leave the room during the presentation
- After the presentation, stay behind, form a circle and answer questions for your guests while your new distributors watch and learn from you.
- Always have a positive attitude at the presentations. Problems always go 'upline' and are not voiced at the presentations.
- Give 'welcome' smiles and handshakes before and after the Presentation.
- Volunteer to help at the registration table, and be courteous to other representatives and their guests.
- Have some of your products ready to sell your prospect sitting next to you at the presentation. You'd be able to sell more

products if they can make an impulse decision than if you have to go to your car and get it.

Equipment to be Used for the Hotel Presentation

- ❑ projector, extension cords, extra bulb, screen slides
- ❑ cash box, receipts, registration signs, guest sign-in sheets, pens and name tags
- ❑ media player and tapes, CDs, or DVDs

Stage or front setup

- ❑ Screen with media player behind the screen
- ❑ Projector

The room must be set up in a 'theatre-style' with the registration table at the entrance into the room or just inside the entrance of the room. The registration table should have the cash box, guest registration sign-in, pens, and name tags on it.

Hall Preparation

- ❑ Ensure the room temperature is moderate.
- ❑ Make sure no light cast is into the screen. Delegate the task to a distributor to ensure there is good lighting in the room during testimonials.
- ❑ Set up an easel at the front left of the room and post the special or upcoming events.
- ❑ Set up a slightly smaller number of chairs than number of guests expected, but have extra chairs stacked at back of room ready in case there's an overflow of guests.
- ❑ Tape the extension cords to floor to prevent people from tripping over them.
- ❑ Wait for the leader's instructions to open the room's door.
- ❑ Assign at least two distributors to handle guest registration sign-in, collect the contribution from distributors, and picking up name tags.

- ❑ Delegate the task of controlling the projector to a distributor to switch the projector light on or off during the presentation.
- ❑ Start music just prior to opening the doors to the room and turn it off just prior to starting the meeting. Turn it back on at the end of the meeting.
- ❑ Assign two distributors to greet the guests with a smile and suggest filling any available front seats.
- ❑ Doors should be closed at the start of meeting and no one should be admitted to the room or go out until the start of testimonials (product and/or business)
- ❑ Always remember to work together as a team. If something needs to be done, address that need right away.

Show Acknowledgement & Recognition to Drive your Business

More than anything else, people will respond to acknowledgement and recognition. During your presentations, acknowledge anyone who qualified for their first step check or first step-3 check in one week, first new distributor or successful home presentation. Recognition inspires the group. The key element when giving recognition is that it must be sincere and for accomplishment.

Change the guard

It may be that, whenever you're having presentations, you will have distributors who attend religiously to get a sense of belongingness or recognition by giving the same testimonial each week.

Change the guard. Have new performers participate and give their testimonial. Oftentimes, the best testimony can be as simple as, "I just started with this company and have already sponsored two friends and have another here with me tonight."

Last but not least, always build for upcoming events. Have something for your guests to look forward to and keep their interest on your business. Who knows, you could just be one follow-up, or presentation away to winning another distributor.

IN-HOME MLM PRESENTATION

The 2-on-1

It is not always possible to get someone out to a scheduled in-home presentation or hotel presentation. A great alternative is a 2-on-1 presentation. This again is easy for you because when done right, your upline does all the work.

The easiest way to do a 2-on-1 presentation is to invite someone for a business presentation either at your home or theirs. Or it could be somewhere 'neutral' like a restaurant.

Your upline should be there as well so he can do the presentation for you, help you with any objections, and share their story. After a successful presentation, your upline should be able to offer support to new distributors.

Based on experience, presentations have a high success rate on the spot because people get their questions answered and are actively engaged during the discussion.

The 1-on-1

If you have to do one, the basic principle of doing a 2-on-1 presentation still applies. In this case, however, you have to do all the work on your own. Whenever possible, inform your upline about your plans, have your upline call you need some questions answered after the presentation.

It's perfectly okay to let them know who you are presenting to and that your upline can speak to them to answer any questions. You want your upline calling in after you are completely done showing the products and plan, so timing is very important.

The easiest way to do a 1-on-1 presentation is to invite someone to your home and show them a presentation on the internet if your company has one which you can use.

Using the internet or some other sales aid to do the presentation for you helps give some kind of a 'third party' validation, although it won't be as good as having an upline doing it for you.

Based on experience, 1-on-1 presentations can be successful mostly in selling products, but not so much convincing people to join after the presentation or have success in sponsoring others.

HANDLING MLM OBJECTIONS

There are several basic steps to follow when addressing and answering objections which can be learned and practiced very easily. When used properly, objections won't be viewed as a problem, but as an opportunity to eliminate underlying concerns, thus enabling you to retailing the product or enrolling a new distributor in your organization.

Basic Steps

1. Listen carefully to your prospect's objection or question and refrain from interrupting or anticipating what they are going to say next. Most of the time your prospect's question or underlying concern is disguised as a sincere objection.

2. Agree with your prospect's objection. Appreciate their reasons for thinking that way, or reiterate their objection so that you could understand clearly what they really meant. Using the words 'feel' or 'found' will usually bring them around to your point of view.

    Example:

    "I understand why you feel that way…"

    "I can truly appreciate what you're saying…"

    "I felt that way myself and when I found out… I got really excited."

    The key here is to avoid provoking the other person's resistance and maintain rapport using key phrases to begin your conversation each time.

Example:

"I agree..."

"I respect..."

and,

"I appreciate..."

followed by an 'and.'

Avoid using 'but' or 'however' as these words might estrange the other person and contribute to disagreement, instead of the agreement that we're looking for. You want your prospect to be at ease, less defensive of their objection and more receptive to you and your response. More importantly, you want to be able to turn your prospect into a new retail customer or distributor and leave them with a feeling that the decision they made was truly their own with the help of your caring guidance.

3. Respond to your prospect's objection or question precisely and in a concise manner. Don't take their objections personally. After a while you'll soon recognize the common objections that recur while doing this in any MLM company. Learn one or two responses for each one to make sure you're always prepared each time these objections crop up.

Once you've answered your prospect's question or concerns, 'tie it all down' and move on. Confirm your prospect understands and agrees with it before proceeding any further with your presentation.

Example:

"Does that answer your question?"

"Does that make sense to you now?"

"Wouldn't you agree?"

4. Once your prospect understands and agrees with your response, always return to a closing question, giving them a choice of things you would like to see them do.

Example:

"Great! Based on what you've seen and heard, how do you see yourself participating in my MLM company – as a retail customer or building a business as a distributor?" (pause and wait for a response)

or,

"Great! Let's get you started with the products, so you can start enjoying the benefits"

and without pausing, continue with,

"Would you prefer to take care of that with a visa or Mastercard?" (pause)

Keep in mind that a strong 'no' at this point in time is way better than an indefinite 'maybe,' which is just a polite way of saying, 'no thanks.'

Handling Objections about the MLM Business

The idea is to be able to tailor the following sample responses to fit any given situation. Preparedness is the key to handling objections about the MLM business.

1. "I've never sold anything in my life – I don't think I can do this."

Psychology:

"Can I do this?" or "I'm afraid of rejection."

Response:

"You don't have to sell anything. If you can ask people if they want to make some extra money and then give them a website, you can do this."

or

"I appreciate how you feel." (agree)

"I felt the same way when I got started." (relate)

"What I found was that it's just like recommending a great restaurant or a good movie to people." (solution)

"You've done that before, haven't you?" (confirmation)

or

"I know how you feel. I felt the same way myself when I started in this business. The thing that got me excited, though, was when I found out that the company's system actually provides the mechanism for the sale – we don't. The online presentation you saw moved you to this point, didn't it? Really, all <distributor's name> has done up to now is direct you to that online presentation, wouldn't you agree? After watching the presentation some people will decide to buy the product while others start distributing it as well." (response)

"Can you see how simple it would be to start developing your own business by doing the same thing?" (confirmation)

THE MLM SUCCESS BIBLE

2. **Is this one of those pyramids?"**

   Response question:

   "What do you mean by a pyramid?"

   Psychology:

   Your prospect is thinking this is an illegal scheme that might get into trouble down the road and they'll have wasted their time and energy. Or, most often they are not referring to something illegal but 'pyramid' is being used as a common terminology of the networking structure. In this case your response could be, "Absolutely! That is why I am so excited about it. Wait till you see how you can make the money."

   Response:

   "I appreciate your concern." (agree)

   "I was worried about the same thing myself until I checked it out. There is no similarity. Pyramids are schemes and rarely have a decent product or service for sale. They promote the recruitment of people and generally demand a high capital investment with no refund policy." (relate)

   "Our program is nothing like that. You can start your business for very little. As a member, you obtain the right to market very exclusive, legitimate memberships and guarantee 100% consumer satisfaction. Our commissions are generated only on the sales volume of these memberships." (solution)

   Much like golf courses sell memberships, so do we.

   "So you can see, it doesn't operate anything like a pyramid, does it? This is one of the finest business opportunities available – wouldn't you agree? (confirmation)

3. **"I am not comfortable approaching my family and friends"**

   Psychology:

   > There is a fear of lack of approval. The prospect has a lack of understanding and belief of the network marketing industry. Their mindset is one of a business attempting to get people instead of trying to give to people. This is why prospects that are given an entire presentation showing the concept of leverage and duplication become interested in the business.

   Response:

   > "I appreciate your concern." (agree)

   > "I was worried about the same thing myself until I saw that all I have to do is refer my friends or family to an online presentation and if they have interest, they will call me." (relate)

4. **"I just don't know many people."**

   Psychology:

   > What they are really saying is "I don't know if any of my friends would be willing to do this." They are prejudging and have a fear of lack of acceptance or rejection.

   Response:

   > "If you can ask people if they would like to make some extra money and refer them to a website, you can do this."

   or

   > "I can appreciate that. That's the beauty of this opportunity. You don't need to know a lot of people. In fact, our compensation

plan is specifically designed for people like you. You can succeed by introducing a few distributors to our program. This company is built on word-of-mouth advertising – you tell a few people, who tell a few more. Our training programs and field support will show you exactly how to build an organization from just a few friends and associates. And I'll be there to help you get started and work with you every step of the way." (agree)

"Do you see how we can make this work together?" (confirmation)

or

Response:

"I think we all feel like that sometimes. I know I've felt that way. I couldn't believe it when I found out that the average person knows upwards of 300 people! Even if you are new in town, you can be successful in our program because you need to sponsor only a few successful people to build a business!"

"Isn't it great to know that ordinary people like us can do this?" (confirmation)

5. **"I really don't have the time to get involved in something like this."**

Psychology:

"Can I do this with the limited time I have and be successful?"

Response:

"If you can make the time to ask people if they would like to make some extra money and then refer them to a website, then you can do this!"

or

"I can understand why you feel that way." (agree)

"I felt that way myself since time is very valuable. I found that by simply asking people if they were on the Internet, if they were making money with the Internet, and if they would be interested in learning more. In a brief conversation, I've been able to stimulate interest. With my sponsor's support, it has led to getting my business off the ground – a business that could give me an income of as much as 1,000 dollars to 2,000 dollars per week and more. Wouldn't you want to take advantage of that?" (relate)

or

Response:

"I felt that way myself but I found it was really a question of priorities. When I considered all the things I was doing and realized that some of them were not taking me where I wanted to be 5 or 10 years from now, I decided it would be wise to dedicate some time each week to doing something to accomplish my goals." (relate)

Confirmation or Response:

"I know how you feel. Time's a hard thing to find these days, isn't it? When I was first introduced to this business I felt it was impossible to squeeze anything else into my schedule. Let me tell you, though, what I found out about the company's system. I found they could show me how to utilize 5 to 10 dead hours a week in the schedule I already had. It was amazing! For example, it took <distributor's name> only a minute or less to refer you to the Online Presentation you just watched, didn't it? Imagine how many times a week you'd have the opportunity to do the same thing? The system does the work for you. You just talk to interested people. In those few hours, following the system can build you a 30,000-dollars-a-week residual income."

or

"Can't you see how quickly we can build this?"

6. **"I want to think it over."**

Psychology:

This is a fear statement. What they are really saying is, "Let me think of why I shouldn't do this," rather than "Why I should do this." With this statement most people will talk themselves out of the business.

Response:

"I agree with you. The more you think of the Internet opportunity being open now, the surer I am you will agree that the timing is right to profit."

or

"I can appreciate that." (agree)

"It's only natural to want to think it over. What I found was that it's not how fast a decision is made that counts, but the accuracy of it – right? Just for my own information, what's the main thing you have to work through in order to make a decision one way or the other?" (relate)

Draw out and answer any questions your prospect has in these areas. Tie down and confirm that each of your responses is a satisfactory answer.

"So the only thing you're really not sure of is how you see yourself fitting into this opportunity. Is that correct? Great! Then let's talk in a few days to see if you are ready to get started."

"Does that make sense to you?" (confirmation)

7. **"I don't have the money."**

Psychology:

The real fear is about losing the money or not making money. To prove the point, if you put a brand new luxury vehicle in their driveway and offer to give it to them if they come up with 2,000 dollars, they would come up with the money. They have not seen enough value in the opportunity to overcome this fear.

Response:

"You can make money by referring people to an online presentation, and it doesn't cost you anything to generate interest."

or

"Oh, I know how you feel. That's a valid concern. I felt the same way myself when I first looked at the company. The truth is, we all have money, don't we? It's just that we have to use it for rent or mortgages, groceries and bills. What I found out was that I always had to pay those bills anyway and every month was the same; I had none left over. But when I used 1,500 of those dollars to start a business for myself, the next month I had something producing some dollars for me, so I didn't have to find as much to pay the bills. Each month as my business grew, it paid more and more of my bills for me, freeing up more of my regular cash flow."

"Wouldn't it be great to have the same thing happen for you?" (confirmation)

8. **"Can't you tell me more about it over the phone?"**

    Psychology:

    What they are really saying is tell me about it so I don't have to look.

    Response:

    "Sure I could. But in all fairness to you, the website presentation can tell you more clearly in a few minutes what would take me a couple of hours. Besides, it would be like me trying to describe what someone looked like to you over the phone. Just look at the video and I'll call you back tomorrow."

    "It'll be easier to talk when we've both seen the same information, wouldn't you agree?" (confirmation)

9. **"I'm not interested!"**

    Psychology:

    They are saying no to something they do not understand.

    Response:

    "I know how you feel. As a matter of fact, I felt exactly the same way myself when someone introduced this to me. What I found out, though, was that while I thought I knew what they had to offer, I couldn't have been more misinformed. What I have to show you is potentially worth 30,000 dollars a week."

"I've never met a serious business person who wasn't interested in making more money or open to other opportunities, have you?" (confirmation)

10. "I know someone who tried this and failed."

Psychology:

They don't believe they can do it. It is a fear of failure.

Response:

"Really? How long did they try? Remember when I showed you leverage? You may only have 10 or less distributors in your network after a few months. But after 8 months you can have thousands!"

or

"Really? How long did they try? They probably didn't fail; they quit. If they would have sponsored just one person per month I am sure they would have had success."

or

"That's true, it happens. In your past experience, though, has there ever been anything that you've been able to do better than him/her? Who's to say you couldn't do better than him/her this time as well? Think of it. Many people fail in small businesses on a daily basis while many others succeed. The difference is quite often not the person but the system they have in place, wouldn't you agree?"

"If you will follow our success system, I can assure you won't fail!" (confirmation)

Prospect's question to distributor:

"How much money do you make?"

Response:

"Nothing yet. I'm just getting started and thought you might want to make it with me. You're one of the first people I thought of."

To Circumvent All Objections at the Beginning, you can simply say:

"I'll bet in your business you have people giving you all kinds of excuses why they can't buy your product or service, don't you? Do you generally find that none of their excuses are valid reasons? Well, it's the same in our business!"

"What reason could you possibly have for not getting started?"

Handling Objections about the MLM Products

Here are some examples on how to deal with objections regarding your products. It is assumed that you've already exhausted every effort to deal with objections regarding the MLM business and you're now trying to retail your product or turn him into a regular buyer.

1. "My religion prevents me from taking part"

Psychology:

Either they really are religious, or they just are looking for an excuse. Either way, let them be.

Response:

"I completely understand and respect that. I wish you well in the future. Maybe one day we can do business together.

2. **"The product is too expensive."**

Psychology:

Usually just looking for a reason to make you go away.

Response:

"May I ask what particular product you're comparing its price to? Because sometimes, it comes down to value rather than the price itself."

"If you want something so bad right then and there, the price didn't matter so much to you, right?" (confirmation)

The strategy is to divert the issue from being too expensive, to their own perception of value. Refresh their memories on how they've been willing to part with their hard-earned money just to get those things that mean a lot to them or have great value to them. They key here is to instill the value of your product to your customers in such a way that price is of little consequence to them.

Part 5

ONGOING INCOME & MLM EDUCATION

WAYS TO EARN AFTER BUILDING YOUR NETWORK

Leveraged Residual Income

Did you know that the average distributor in MLM or network marketing makes less than 2,000 dollars per year, and that those people earning these numbers per year are actually getting richer doing it?

How could this be possible? Let's take a look at how much money you would need to have to invest and make 2,000 dollars a year.

Simple interest at 10% means you would need 20,000 dollars in the bank, or rather a fairly sizable investment as most banks won't pay you 10% these days. Suppose you make 3% interest in a bank account? Using simple interest, you would need 66,666 dollars and 66 cents in the bank just to earn 2,000 dollars for one year.

Let's throw in tax to this scenario and see what happens. A network marketer earning 2,000 dollars a year through his MLM or network marketing business can deduct business expenses to a point where he is able to earn a tax refund of around 2,000 dollars a year while earning that same amount of money.

In other words, 2,000 dollars a year of residual income and another 2,000-dollar tax refund. Unbelievable? Ask your accountant how a home-based business can help you take advantage of it.

However, it doesn't mean the expenses of your MLM business, per se, are the reasons for getting the tax refund. The truth when it comes to tax laws is that those business expenses are probably made up mostly with money you're already spending even if you didn't have a home-based business.

A portion of your automobile and home, for instance, can qualify as expenses. The thing is, you pay for those two things whether you have a home-based business or not.

How about the one with 66,666 dollars and 66 cents tied up in savings bonds or some other 'ultra safe' investment? Unfortunately, they don't get any tax breaks on it unless it is in some kind of RRSP or 401K plan. Worse still, they have to pay about 50% in taxes to the government as is the case with most countries where passive income is taxed at the highest rates.

So what should be your income goals in your business? As we have seen, even a 200-dollar monthly residual income is a life-changing financial goal. Start small, dream big, and work towards your goal.

Isn't it ironic that the price of not doing MLM is much more expensive than actually doing it? Take action, set your goal today and start going after it.

Retailing Products with an MLM Software

It seems MLM companies are doing their best to ensure you don't ever have to retail. The truth is, if the MLM company you're currently in doesn't have a retail aspect of running the business or somehow be able to move product to end users outside of the network instead of just business builders themselves, it's probably one of those companies at risk of being shut down by regulators.

Melelauca seemed to be the closest MLM company to not require retailing at first glance. However, they were able to get around this because a lot of their members have stated their interest in just being customers in their paper works.

This, perhaps, is what keeps them 'legal' without causing people to buy bottles of products they don't need and sell it to others. They just sign up the new person as a customer and have that person buy directly from the company – a good model as it seems to be tried and true.

Companies who write explicitly that members never need to retail anything are likely to be struck down by the regulators just about the time when they're big enough to pay members big paychecks.

Tread very carefully with companies that openly promotes on not needing to retail any products trying to get you in. More so if those companies don't have any autoship or purchase requirement at all as they are likely to go nowhere.

MLM software like the ones offered at Internet Nextstep allows you to use your replicated website to sell products to people and have them shipped to them. Your account is credited with the retail markup and your customer gets the products shipped directly from the company.

When you have retailed enough products that it exceeds your autoship point requirement, the system can be set by you to cancel your autoship for any months that you are qualified through retail sales.

The best part here is that your retail customers can also set themselves up on an autoship. If you are able to retail just enough, you will never need to purchase yourself if you don't want to, although we strongly suggest that you use the products and services of your company and be committed enough to have any chance of success. Keep in mind that your own testimonial is always the best one.

Retailing or selling of products and services to the end-user is required by law in any company and prevents them from being labeled as a pyramid. Next time you come across these companies who promote that you don't need selling, ask yourself if such companies could stand long enough, or if you can actually earn residual income from it.

Residual Income through Your MLM Website

Having your own website to propagate your MLM business and monetize your web content is probably one of the best ways to generate ongoing residual income even after you've already established your MLM network.

Every time a new client comes in and goes into the process of creating content and working on SEO, we want to monetize that effort by doing a few things while preparing that site to be indexed by Google. Once done, we can then start sending traffic to it and monetize our efforts with Google AdSense.

Setting up Your MLM Website and Blog

First of all, we need to meet Google's standards by setting up a blog which uses the same key words as our chosen domain. For instance, weset up a blog for Roatan Cluband wrote introductory entries, or a 'play-by-play' of what the company does in order to get some things indexed by Google. This was then linked to our target domain.

The Roatan Club site was linked to a a membership platform formore information specific to the clients' offers. These can be spread out in many places while maintaining its quality.

While uploading the site, we can install a SiteMap generator script into our site and verify this with Google Sitemaps (this allows websites to be listed faster with Google). Once again, we want to keep Google satisfied by using as many Google tools as we can.

Finally, we will be able get AdSense into these pages initially in a totally unrestricted format. While starting with a content-rich site, we are not too concerned about 'feeding' our competition. We are more interested in keeping Google satisfied and generating some income in the process.

Giving Google Adsense the heads up on your new site would somehow give them some incentive to index your site as soon as possible. This way, Google can start earning money through your website, and you, as the site owner, can start earning off of Google. It's a win-win situation.

However, the strategy is slightly different if we are dealing with a deep-seated site in Google for a client, as is the case with Internet Nextstep (internetnextstep.com). Preferably, we refer to sites by domain names, giving them the all-important link-ins should people find our blog entries be useful and thought it good to link to them.

With established sites, we take a look at the web statistics for a specific site and identify which pages have the biggest traffic. These pages will be evaluated whether or not they are core to the sites' customers, or if they are just additional content-rich pages not directly involved in the sales process or recruitment of clients.

It is strongly advised to place Google Adsense into pages that are 'high-traffic.' However, these pages should not involve critical decision-making processes to avoid causing too much fatigue to the clients.

Once we have our Google AdSense in place, we can start to, yet again, give play-by-plays in our Blogger Blogs, as well as our B2Evolution blogs on site. They're posted in both locations, although slightly different from each other.

Mentioning URLs added to Google AdSense to these posts will create traffic to the sites, possibly from those people looking to find something they like from our clients' site like the Roatan Club. Or if not, then possibly some people who finds interest in a Google ad and clicked it.

Integrating Google AdSense to Blog Entries

People who are still new to the business don't realize how much residual income they can earn potentially by monetizing their website. Oftentimes, they would think that AdSense is helping the competition by redirecting traffic to them. As we already know our long-term gains from using this free service is far greater than what competitors would initially have.

Here are four steps on how you can use AdSense on your blogs to their fullest:

Step 1. Prioritize on using or creating 'high-traffic' pages. Choose a page or two on your site, or make a new site that enables you to get traffic high enough to warrant adding Google Adsense. Go to Google and Register for a Google AdSense account. It would take around 48 hours, or so, to get the approval.

Step 2. Create Google AdSense code for your site. Familiarize yourself with the process of creating Google Adsense code and how to properly use it to your site. You can find some great tutorials about Google Adsense over the Internet.

Step 3. Integrate the Adsense code to your site. Paste the code block generated by Google AdSense into your site. Observe proper placement so as not to distract your customers.

Step 4. Beat the competition. Now that you are set, you can proceed on cutting down your competitors. Internet Nextstep, one of the leading providers of email marketing, MLM, and affiliate-type membership software, implemented this on its own site (internetnextstep.com). Google AdSense was used extensively on blogs and other 'high-traffic' pages except the main product pages. While this would earn less money for the company, not monetizing the main pages will actually help keep the clients focused.

Internet Nextstep has an extensive free MLM training section where Google AdSense has been used on its free MLM training pages. This enabled the company to earn residual income from just a few dollars a day during the first few days.

With regards to proper placement of Google AdSense, clients can use their own discretion. Generally, we like to do similar steps depending on where a client is in the process.

LEARNING MORE ABOUT THE MLM BUSINESS

Second Life Virtual MLM World

What if we can create a virtual word where network marketers can experiment, learn, and put their prospecting skills to the test without spending on anything except their time and a stable internet connection?

The good news is, it's already been made – the virtual world of MLM called the *Second Life*.

There are an unlimited number of potential prospects joining *Second Life* daily. Learn how to do things right and you could certainly find a few of them who would like to be on your team.

The great part is, you won't have to invest on anything except your time. If you have a high-speed internet connection and a midrange computer or laptop, you can enjoy the benefits of joining this amazing virtual MLM community.

Just like in real world, network marketers go through a certain process in *Second Life* to be certified as an MLM networker which involves:

- Creating an account
- Attend an orientation in *Second Life*
- Attend the INS MLM Training Institute
- Explore the virtual world of *Second Life*
- Start finding prospects

Second Life as a Virtual Training Ground

Here is how you could use Second Life to gain valuable prospects.

Get in the game, take a tour, and meet people. Don't go around spouting your MLM business opportunity to people. Start by making friends. Once you've made a relationship, you can eventually talk about what you do for a living and in your spare time.

Be as natural as you can be. Otherwise, you will find yourself banned from many lands for being obnoxious. You still apply the 3-foot rule prospecting, only this time, it's made into 3-inche or 7-centimetre prospecting! The good thing with *Second Life* is that you're in disguise, and you don't have to meet real people face to face. It can all be done from your computer with a broadband connection to the Internet.

Once you've met someone, you could get 'out-of-world' information to link up about your opportunity should they become interested. Or, get yourself the ability to do a presentation 'in-world.'

There's a great BizOpp mall under construction that will give you the ability to upload your presentation and have it available 24 hours per day 'in-world.' It's a great way to have people you meet learn more about you.

You could also get more involved in the game and rent some space to put your own house, castle, or anything that you can imagine. Make it big and put your own presentation room in it. Use your own creativity.

As you grow, you may want to have your own *Second Life* location so you won't just have the ability to have a scripted presentation, but you can also have a live voice broadcast presentation in a presentation room. Imagine a virtual world where after the presentation people can come up to you and ask questions just like in the real world.

How NOT to Spend Time in Second Life

Basically all the necessary manners in real life should be used in *Second Life* as well. We don't approach people we don't know and spew out our business opportunity all over them. Lucky for them, in *Second Life*, prospects can block, mute and 'teleport' to happier places.

MLM is a great industry, and done right, it could lead to a lot of friends and some extra money. *Second Life* and MLM go hand in hand to help shy people hide behind an avatar and reach out to strangers.

Done right, *Second Life* contacts could earn a fortune for MLM networkers. Make friends first and start nurturing relationship. Eventually you could start talking about business.

Or, they will ask to come and see your *Second Life* space. Set it up and use it to tell your MLM Story. There are lots of things you could do to make it soft sell the opportunity.

Do it right, and you'll make a fortune; do it wrong, and you'll find yourself in the same mess in *Second Life* as much as you'll do in real life.

MLM University Training

I learned of the MLM University Training format in the very first MLM company I was a distributor for. They deducted a training fee off of our first four checks to cover the 250-dollar training fee at the time.

Once I had finished paying my 250-dollar fee, I couldn't wait for the next MLM University to begin. I wasn't hating the mandatory deduction at all.

The format was outstanding. Two corporate trainers took turns segment by segment. These were high ranking distributors within the company, not just paid resource speakers. It was a 2-day event which fell on a Saturday and Sunday. A night before, there would be an evening event for those who qualified by some sponsoring type of contest leading up to the MLM University event.

The two days of training was a combination of a deep dive on the commission plan, a deep dive on the products, and a whole bunch of general MLM training and objection-handling. The training also got into Goal-Setting and List-Making along with their approaches.

What's very creative about the whole concept was that the corporate trainers, as they were called, were flown in, and put up in a hotel at the companies' expense. They were also paid a 2000-dollar stipend each for doing the training.

Once you've advanced far enough in the company, they'd start bringing you inside and suggest that you may want to become a trainer yourself. You should have already earned real money in the company, and the respect of your group while doing so to qualify.

In the first few MLM University Trainings, they did, there were not any corporate trainers, so they had help from some qualified outsiders, and that served as the springboard to gain interest of leaders to be trained to become MLM University corporate trainers.

At one time, the company had MLM Universities going every single weekend all over Canada and the USA.

My goal was to have over half the room in my down line. The last MLM University the company did, I had 82 people. Such is the power of MLM training and the power of goals.

It had such an amazing impact on my MLM career that I have been saddened over the past 6 years that most clients just didn't seem interested in taking on such a format of official training.

It's good to know that this is no longer the case. Many more clients, as well as non-client companies, are starting to adopt the old, proven principles of MLM University style training once again.

Part 6

**KEEPING YOUR EYES
ON THE PRIZE**

THE ROATAN CONNECTION

*An MLM partnership that started
in friendship ten years ago*

I just want to share a story with you about why networking is the most wonderful thing to be involved with on the planet when done right.

About 10 years ago, I agreed to a cup of coffee with a fellow who had responded to my fax I had sent out looking for folks interested in a business opportunity.

Upon meeting, we both realized we were very focused on our respective opportunities and decided to just be friends. Right. You're thinking, it never happened – it did. We became friends, and respected each other's business for many years.

In fact this fellow is of such high integrity, that when the business I was with failed, and started a new division that I was offered the top spot in, he recommended it was best to take that opportunity, rather than pouncing on me to do his business.

Well in the end, I did end up involved in his business. Worked it for a bit, but it just wasn't a fit. We became closer and closer as friends.

Now my friend is off to retire in Roatan Honduras. Strange. My second friend I have lost to that Island – there must be something up with that!

Here is where the story gets interesting. We now make MLM Software as our faithful followers know, and this fellow continues to work in the same MLM company he has been with for 10 or more years.

As he moves to Roatan Honduras, he has been sharing with me the business opportunity in real estate there. I have always been intrigued but very skeptical as I have watched his involvement over the past number of years.

He approached me the other day with an unique business opportunity in real estate that our MLM Software kernel can help. It is not MLM but rather a community concept. Very interesting.

Ten or more years after agreeing to be friends, we will now be in business together as Internetnextstep.com starts to provide services for this new Roatan Real Estate business.

The point? Treat people with respect that you meet while building your MLM as life is long and business connections are business connections. We will now do some real business together after meeting for that fateful day for a completely different reason.

I love networking and all the hidden rewards it provides.

THE PAIN AND PLEASURE OF PROSPECTING

by Jack Rosen

Have you ever procrastinated?

Yes? Good. (I was afraid I was the only one.) So why do you think you and I do that? I think I know--we procrastinate because we associate more pain with the process of doing than we do pleasure from achieving the result.

Maybe you put off cleaning out the garage, because you perceived a greater pleasure in watching a football game. Or perhaps you procrastinated for so long that it eventually became easier--less painful--to just take action and complete the task. For example, if it takes a half an hour every time you try to find something in the garage and your spouse is constantly on your back about getting it straightened up, the thought of not cleaning the garage is probably more painful than actually cleaning it.

When I was an aircraft mechanic, my boss would spend three hours trying to avoid some work that would have taken him less than an hour to do! When I realized what he was doing, I also realized how frequently I have been guilty of the same behavior. My boss stood for everything I didn't want to be--the thought of bearing any similarity to him was so painful to me, I did everything I could do to eliminate it from my life.

The pain associated with thinking that I might be like him forced me to change my actions--proof once again that we are emotional creatures, not logical ones. We mostly act on our emotions and then rationalize our actions with logic and thought. Didn't you fall in love with your car and then rationalize how you could stretch to pay for it? Did you do the same thing with your house? You fell in love with it and then rationalized how you would pay for it, or figured out a way to fix it up. The controlling force in our lives is almost always pain or pleasure.

Before we take a look at how this applies to Network Marketing, here is another illustration of the point: Have you ever been on a diet or started an exercise program? Why did you go on that diet or start exercising? Was it to look better, or feel better physically and emotionally? Maybe you wanted to fit more lithely into your clothes, be sexier and even live longer?

Why did you stop?

The pain you associated with your actions was greater than the pleasure you might get in the future. What I mean is, the pain of going to the gym every day and not eating the foods you like now, was greater than the pleasure of feeling better or being healthier later. Besides, you probably thought you would put all that weight back on anyway.

Part of the problem is that we have all become accustomed to instant gratification. It used to take two hours to make dinner, but nowadays we stand in front of the microwave urging it to hurry up. Think of the pleasure you would get from opening a box of Godiva chocolates and eating a rich piece of mouth-watering dark Swiss-mocha-mousse after facing something frustrating. That instant pleasure is what most people think about. They don't think about how fat it would make them, or how their arteries would clog up. Their first thought is of the pleasure. People whose first thought is the pain will not eat it.

Now let's talk about how this relates to your Network Marketing business (although everything you do is business related). Like Zig Ziglar says, "You have to be before you can do, and you have to do before you can have."

Prospecting is perhaps the biggest area of procrastination for people in this business. And when you look at it in terms of the pain/pleasure paradigm, it's certainly understandable. How much pain is there for you in prospecting someone? You might experience rejection, humiliation, or feel like a failure-- yes? Don't forget the commandment that was drilled into our minds as children: "Never talk to strangers."

Note that the pain itself does not prevent us from acting. It's the fear of pain, or as the familiar acronym says, F.E.A.R.--False Expectations Appearing Real. The pain is not real at that point, it's only our perception of the pain that seems real to us. We feel fear when we turn a negative memory or association into an expectation.

On the other hand, what causes desire? Again, it's a memory or an association that becomes an expectation.

Sound familiar? The definitions are the same. Why do some people fear jumping out of an airplane or riding roller coasters while others desire it? It all depends on whether we associate the activity with pain or pleasure. Most people spend more time avoiding pain than they do seeking pleasure.

Do you?

Here's an example of how you can gradually replace negative associations with positive ones:

A couple of weeks ago I had a friend over to my house. He was deathly afraid of cats. I have two cats in my home, one of which is big, fat, old, all-very-black, utterly beautiful and extremely friendly. His name is Ace. He wants to say hello to everyone. He thinks he owns the house and has to check everybody out. Hey, it's his house! Even if Ace is on the other side of the room, my friend would be pinned to the opposite corner in fear.

In an effort to help him get over his fear, I asked him to pet Ace. He laughed and said, "No way!" While we were discussing the cat, I also started talking about different subjects to break his state of fear. We talked about what it would be like for him to become a Diamond Executive, then back to the cat, and back to the business, and back to the cat. He didn't realize that I was doing this deliberately.

I asked him what he thought would happen to him if he did pet the cat. He said that he thought he would literally die. He really was deathly afraid. I put the cat on my lap and told him that it would feel like his fur hat. He also mentioned to me that when he was a child his mother had a fur blanket that he used to lie on. I got him to associate pleasurable memories to cats. To make a long story short, he petted Ace and he didn't die. Now it doesn't bother him when Ace is in the room. Although they may never be the best of friends, he felt so good that he'd faced and conquered his fears by reinforcing his positive associations with the cat. Each of us has much more control over our associations than most people think.

One of my fears is drowning, yet I am an avid scuba diver. The reason is that I don't associate scuba diving with drowning. I associate it with freedom. Freedom is also one of the reasons that I got involved with Network Marketing. When I am diving, I am totally free. I am weightless; I can move in three dimensions, I have no mortgage payment or any bills, no upline or downline. In fact, I have only the moment and the beauty that surrounds me. I associate so much pleasure with diving that the only pain associated with it is the pain if I don't go.

I've also had a fear of bridges for a long time. I couldn't go over a bridge without envisioning my car going over the rail and into the water. Now I look forward to driving across a bridge, because I have associated it with something fun, like a roller coaster ride.

How much pleasure is there in prospecting someone? Maybe you experience pleasure in having accomplished something, or maybe you find pleasure in overcoming a fear. We could take pleasure in knowing that we are closer to our goals, or that we can help someone reach theirs.

But as we all know, pleasure is usually not enough to overcome fear. Since the fear of pain is stronger than the desire for pleasure--like the fear of loss is stronger than the desire to gain--you have to think of it differently.

To slightly change your perspective, ask yourself how much pain is there in not prospecting somebody?

Think about the fact that every prospect you don't approach just said "No" to the business. The result is exactly the same. Think of what you might lose. You could have just lost $100,000 per year. If you don't prospect, you may lose your new home, sexy car, your chance at early retirement. You also just denied yourself the opportunity to live the lifestyle you've always dreamt about.

These are also the pleasurable things that you will gain. If your belief system is strong, you will also realize what you just cost your prospect by not sharing what you know about this business. How would you have liked it if no one ever told you about Network Marketing? Associate so much pain with not prospecting, that you will have no choice but to prospect!

Think about the fact that every prospect you don't approach just said 'No' to the business. The result is exactly the same

I used to say that we are not responsible for our first thought. We grew up in a negative society and are conditioned so our first reaction is one of negativity. If you don't think we're affected by conditioning, let me give you a few examples!

Have you ever had to go to the store on your way home from work, but instead of turning toward the store, you turned toward home as if you were on auto pilot? Did you ever see anyone eat a lemon and your mouth waters just looking at them? Why are yawns contagious? How do you spell relief? Most people's first thought is ROLAIDS, but it's not. It's r-e-l-i-e-f. I bet you can think of many more examples of our conditioning.

Since we are now learning to be positive thinkers, what about that second thought? We are totally responsible for that thought.

If negative conditioning is keeping you from your goals, ask yourself, what action will I take after receiving that first thought? Will it be negative or positive? Will it be fight or flight? In order to make a decision, you must think of both outcomes and what you truly want. You must make a decision, and you must act upon a commitment to follow through. The follow-through action might be one of taking no action at all. This whole process might take just a fraction of a second.

The challenge here is that you have to think about it. What if your first thought is to prospect this person? What if fear, and pain, were not even associated with prospecting? What if prospecting were pleasurable and fun, right from the first thought? Would you have any problem doing it then?

But how do you get to that point?

You've probably heard some top income earners say that action cures fear. Well, it absolutely does! If you actively prospect enough times, eventually you won't be scared. However, if you don't want to wait that long, you can change it right now---this minute! Start associating so much pleasure with prospecting that you can't wait to do it.

I make it a game. To me, prospecting is fun because I find people fascinating. I love to see how they react. I'm just waiting for somebody to do something new. Usually they don't do or say anything I haven't seen or heard before.

Didn't you used to play jokes on people when you were a kid? Didn't you ever ring somebody's doorbell and run? Wasn't it fun? Now, did you run completely away or did you just run far enough to hide behind a bush so that you could witness their reaction? That's what I associate prospecting with, something fun.

You see, my first thought is not one of pain. It's one of pleasure. Because I'm human, I don't do that 100 percent of the time, so naturally I'm still working on it and growing. What I have been able to accomplish is that if it's not my first thought, I quickly link the pain of not prospecting to my second thought--how I would feel if I let this opportunity slip away and what I might lose if I don't follow through.

Let's do an exercise: Here are four questions. Please, be completely honest with yourself. Nobody else has to see this. Write down a list and make it as long as possible. This will put some leverage on your side to help you change your prospective. Really get into it and allow yourself to feel the emotions associated with these questions. I'll help you with some of the answers I've heard, but please add your own personal touch to this list.

1. What is the pain I've associated with prospecting in the past? Rejection, humiliation, feel like a failure, uncomfortable, loss of a friendship, lack of approval, etc.

2. What is the pleasure I took from not following through in the past? Don't say "nothing." There are things, just think. Comfortable, secure, more TV time, certainty, no rejection, no change, etc.

3. What will it cost me if I don't follow through now? Make it hurt! I want you to associate so much pain with not following through that it really, really hurts. How does it make you feel not to have these things for you and your family? What kind of person would let that happen? Visualize what it would be like without them! No early retirement, no freedom, fewer friends, no peace of mind, no success, no new home or car, no time with family, debts will increase, no $100,000 or more income per year, no self-respect or self-esteem, no way of achieving goals, no growth, won't be able to help anyone else, etc.

4. What pleasure will I now associate with prospecting? Make a game out of it, see who on the team can get the most no's, have fun with people, success, choices, freedom, fun, personal satisfaction, helping others, self-respect and respect from others, etc.

A lot of this boils down to knowing what you want, and knowing how badly you want it.

A lot of people are "relatively happy," which means that they're not unhappy enough to make themselves actually do anything. We need to hit some sort of bottom, an emotional bottom. Everybody has a different "bottom." The bottom is yours and can be whenever you decide. It must be a bottom that will compel you to act.

I'm trying to bring you there now. Some alcoholics hit bottom when they are living on the streets cleaning windshields with old newspapers and begging for money to get another bottle. Some hit their "bottom" when they total their new Ferrari. They can't get any lower in their minds, and that's when they decide to act. Some never make it and die drunks.

Do you want to die where you are now, or do you want to make a difference? You can create a "bottom" for yourself by realizing that you have a choice right now. There are no circumstances or excuses, because no matter where you are or what you are doing, there is something that you can do now to make it better--if you want to. Are the actions you're taking getting you the results you want? You can think of the movie Network and say to yourself, "I'm mad as hell and I'm not going to take it anymore!"

Or you can be like Popeye and say, "That's alls I can stands and I can't stands n'more." Then what did he do? He broke out a can of spinach, ate it, and then took massive action to accomplish his goal.

There are no circumstances or excuses, becasue no matter where you are or what you are doing, there is something that you can do now to make it better-- if you want to.

There's a lot to be learned from Popeye. For starters, spinach is good for you. Does it really give you super-human strength? What was that spinach actually? Wasn't it a psychological trigger he used to break out of the state he was in? Wasn't it something to interrupt his negative thought pattern of procrastination, helplessness, no self-worth, anger and frustration? Didn't Popeye use it to trigger positive emotions of high self-esteem, power, success, contribution, and action?

He decided when to eat the spinach. He could have eaten it right at the beginning of the show and avoided all of the trouble in the first place. Of course, then there wouldn't be any cartoon and I wouldn't be writing this right now. (Thanks, Popeye!)

The point is, he hit bottom. He decided when that bottom was, snapped himself out of it and took action.

Can't you do that, too? You bet you can, anytime you choose. In this case I'm only talking about prospecting, but you can do this in any area of your life and business. You can change the four questions to relate to doing follow-ups, dieting, exercising, getting to work on time--anything you would want to improve.

Can we get our downline or other people to act? No! Only they can.

It is our job to help them realize when there's a problem and present the solution. You already know that pain can be a greater motivator than pleasure, so go ahead, create some pain, help bring them to their "bottom." Normally, you might ask a prospect what it is they want by asking the question, "If time and money meant nothing to you, what would you be doing now?" How about asking instead, "What are some of the things in life you really want that you're not getting now--or have no way of obtaining with what you're currently doing?"

Create some pain--and then some value. Some people don't know they have a problem. Ask probing questions and actually listen to their answers. The reasons you became a Network Marketer might or might not be the same for your prospects. They have the problem and your opportunity is the bridge to their solution. Are the actions they are currently taking going to solve their problems? I doubt it! What about your downline--are they taking the actions necessary to solve their problems? If not, find out their pain and pleasure.

How about you? Are you taking the actions necessary to solve your problems? If not, why not? What association with pain is holding you back?

Don't be confused. Going to personal growth seminars and listening to tapes and reading books is not the action that will build your business. Yes, it is great to get all of the personal growth that you can. I truly believe that this is a personal growth business with a compensation plan attached. I know, that may sound contradictory, however, many people use personal growth to hide out. The pain of personal growth is less than the pain of doing the business.

Here's the choice it comes down to for a lot of people: Not doing anything at all is too painful to deal with, doing the business is too painful also and so is personal growth. Whichever action is least painful is the one they will choose. It's like water or electricity, they will take the path of least resistance. Every good personal growth trainer will tell you the importance of action, and in Network Marketing (and, I think, everything else, too) that means talking to people--that's how you will build your business.

It is up to you to decide when you "can't stands n'more." You can do it any time you want and it's easy. Find something that will be a psychological triggering device, something that when you see it or touch it, reminds you of the action you need to take. Every time I need some motivation, I reach for a coin that I got last year at a leadership conference. The main subjects were action and belief. The day was filled with energy and I was in a state of excitement and enthusiasm. I've kept this coin with me since that day. It anchors me and helps me associate the appropriate feelings that I need to do this business. I can change my state just by reaching in my pocket, grabbing and fingering that coin.

Another little pointer: Change your physiology. Sit up tall, breath deep. Try this: Plant a huge grin on your face. Too small? Make it bigger. Hold it! Now, without changing your expression at all, become depressed. You can't do it, because your mind and body would be in conflict.

How do depressed people look? Don't they have their heads down, shoulders and backs slumped, faces limp, shallow breathing? If you walked around like that long enough, you would have no choice except to be depressed.

Try walking with the posture of a successful person. Make a 10-day commitment to do it and see what happens. Model a successful person. Think of some of the top income earners in your company, what do they act like? When you take on the physical posture of a positive, successful person, you will also attract more people to you. Give it a try--it works and it's fun to do.

Some people have told me all this "sounds like brainwashing." Well, aren't you and I already brainwashed? All I'm saying is, as long as we're brainwashed, I want to be the one scrubbing my brain. Call it what you will, but it is really just reconditioning. The way I look at it, I'd been working two full-time jobs for five years and getting nowhere. Maybe my brain needed a little washing!

Jack Rosen is a full-time Car Qualified Distributor with N/A/T/O International. He sponsored into the company in 1999, from a career as an Aircraft Technician. He lives with his wife Claire--a Contracts Administrator for a large aerospace company--in Waldwick, NJ.

"THINK AND GROW RICH"

Is it really possible to *'Think and Grow Rich'*? Have you ever given any thought about it? It somewhat comes from the concept of 'anything you can believe, you can achieve.' When you want something so bad and work hard enough for it, you can have virtually anything you want.

A quote from one of my favorite books fits perfectly: 'The price of success has to be paid in full in advance'. No truer words have ever been written. The biggest issue with most people involved in MLM including those who are not MLM is that they give up way to easily.

Just because you can run 5,279 feet in three minutes, doesn't guarantee that you can run a mile in four minutes. Even if a mile is just 5,280 feet, you could pretty much stop short and turn around 12 inches away from the finish line. I have seen this a lot in both small business owners and network marketers. Giving up '12 inches away' from their payday.

A book written by Napoleon Hill deals on this subject of thinking and growing rich in exquisite detail. *'Think and Grow Rich'* is a wonderful book appropriately named as the subject it deals with.

Think and Grow Rich by Napoleon Hill has to be one of my favorite books of all time. I have read the book 10 or 12 times, and I get something new out of it every single time.

It's just so amazing how the contents from the book still holds true today even if it's written way back in the 1930's. The depth of research into the lives of the wealthy is so stunning, yet it still makes for a very entertaining read.

'Thoughts are Things' is probably one of my favorite principles taught in *Think and Grow Rich*. One of the stories tells about how a huge steel company merger all started because of one famous person in history who had the thought that it was possible. From that 'thought' millions of dollars were created, and the person who originally had the thought's wildest imagination achieved wealth. It's just amazing.

Another favorite thought from Napoleon Hill, which is probably the most famous worldwide, tells us that 'Whatever the mind can conceive and believe, it can achieve.' The general principal is there – powerful and true.

This book is a 'must-have' for your library whether you are in MLM or network marketing, or you are just on the path to self-improvement.

DON'T GIVE UP ON YOUR DREAMS
Keith Fiala's journey to music stardom

Keith Fiala tells us his experience as a professional musician and trumpet artist, and recalls his own struggles to fulfill his lifelong dream.

"Ever since I was a little boy, I've known in my heart that I wanted to be a professional trumpet player. Pretty much everyone discouraged the idea because 'the music business is tough to break into,' I was told."

"Even after receiving a full-ride scholarship to UT, Austin to study with Raymond Crissara, I was told, 'You won't last'. After my second semester at UT, I received a letter from the University stating that my 'full-ride' scholarship funding had been pulled by the Texas Legislature to help keep 'instate' kids in-state, and undergrad 'out-of-staters' paying some or full tuition."

"Being young, and hearing all my life that music was a bad choice, I too believed that music was too hard to break in to. So I set out into the world, and found a steady 'day job.' Finding myself locked into a career with a LD telephone provider and NOT playing at all, I was miserable! I gave up my "BIG" dream to become just another worker bee in a huge hive we call society."

"Two years of this 'worker bee syndrome' went by before I even looked at my trumpet again. Feeling lost, miserable, and out of sorts, I began to incorporate practice into my daily routine again. About a year later, I was auditioned to join a band just starting out that would play R&B, Funk, and Soul called Memphis Train. I was hired!"

"Nine years later, this band would become the mainstay of my income, and help me realize my lifelong dream! I AM a full time professional trumpet player and private instructor! How? I was given an article about a man in Desoto, TX by the name of Clint 'Pops'

McLaughlin. He was a private teacher able to help trumpet players fix 'high note' problems."

"My first session with Pops was a 4-hour long butt kicker! But come to find out, the biggest hurdle I had to overcome, was my state of mind. I believed that I was no good, and that I couldn't do what I really wanted to do but refused to give up. Since changing my outlook, I have more than exceeded my playing goals, and have set new standards for myself!"

5 SIMPLE RULES:

1. NEVER give up - failure comes when you stop trying!
2. Be nice, but not a pushover - no one likes to work with an ego-maniac or a whiny child!
3. Think Positive - reach for solutions, don't dwell on problems!
4. Humor & Laughter = a smile. I have fixed more problems with a smile than I could shake a stick at!
5. Eat your vegetables.

- Keith Fiala

CONCLUSION

As you set forth in this exciting journey of multi-level marketing, always remember to look back and learn from all your MLM engagements. Mistakes are inevitable, but what matters is that we don't make them as an excuse for failing. Even the best networkers has had some missteps too, going from one MLM company to another, losing money, and being estranged from people dear to them. But they didn't go out and complain about MLM. Instead, they regarded their past experiences as part of the real life MLM training which is all but necessary to grow and become the successful networkers that they are.

Multi-level marketing as a business model is far from being perfect. Compensation plans may need some revisions to address certain loopholes. MLM trainings may have to be standardized, and more books should be written about the topic to educate people about MLM. Who knows, one of these days, you could be one of those who were able to come up with a more innovative and ingenious way to further enhance how the industry works and create your own MLM company?

It is our earnest hope that this book has been worthwhile and that we are able to equip you with the right tools to start your own MLM network and guide you throughout your efforts. Before we finally draw to a close, it's worth noting that no amount of training or depth of understanding that will ever substitute to one's unwavering and unbending resolve to pursue his dreams and to keep his eyes on the prize. Successful networkers earning their six figures on a regular basis didn't grow rich by just writing or reading books about MLM; they worked on it. They made it to the top, and so can you.

"Action supersedes everything."